SALADS

over 200 mouthwatering step-by-step recipes

SALADS

over 200 mouthwatering step-by-step recipes

STEVEN WHEELER

HERMES HOUSE

This edition is published by Hermes House

Hermes House is an imprint of Anness Publishing Ltd
Hermes House, 88–89 Blackfriars Road, London SE1 8HA
tel. 020 7401 2077; fax 020 7633 9499; info@anness.com

A CIP catalogue record for this book is available from the British Library.

Publisher: Joanna Lorenz
Senior Editor: Joanne Rippin
Designer: Bill Mason
Illustrator: Anna Koska
Editorial reader: Richard McGinlay
Production controller: Ann Childers

Previously published as *Best-Ever Salads*

1 3 5 7 9 10 8 6 4 2

NOTES
For all recipes, quantities are given in both metric and imperial measures and, where appropriate,
measures are also given in standard cups and spoons.
Follow one set, but not a mixture, because they are not interchangeable.

Standard spoon and cup measurements are level.
1 tsp = 5ml, 1 tbsp = 15ml, 1 cup = 250ml/8fl oz

Australian standard tablespoons are 20ml. Australian readers should use 3 tsp in place of 1 tbsp for
measuring small quantities of gelatine, cornflour, salt, etc.

Medium eggs (US large) should be used unless otherwise stated.

CONTENTS

INTRODUCTION

Introduction

A well-made salad is almost lyrical in its combination of fresh tastes, textures and colours. This book looks at a large variety of salad themes and shows that there is far more to salads than meets the eye.

Seasonal changes are important and provide a useful lead when you are searching for inspiration. The finest salads begin with one or two ingredients that may catch the attention. If you come across a butter-rich pear, partner it with a handful of toasted pecan nuts and a few leaves of young spinach and combine with a blue cheese dressing. If a freshly boiled crab takes your fancy, consider the rich flavours of avocado, coriander leaves and lime. Some new potatoes and young lettuce leaves will make it a salad to remember.

Most salads fit into the summer season and are inspired by an abundance of freshness and colour. Summer salads are wonderful if eaten out of doors. In autumn and winter we move inside to enjoy the warm flavours of wild mushrooms, duck breast and chicken livers. The richness of these ingredients combines well with hearty leaves of oakleaf lettuce, escarole and chicory. Spring sees the arrival of young vegetables and tender salad leaves: corn salad, spinach and rocket. These delicate flavours marry best with simply-grilled fish, eggs, ham and chicken. In fact, simplicity is the key to a successful salad: where two or more ingredients combine, their flavours should blend well together but should also still be identifiable.

Whether you want a snack or a full meal, a side dish or celebratory feast, this book has a salad for every occasion. There are cooked and uncooked salads using a vast range of vegetables, pasta, rice, fish, meat, poultry and fruit, all of them mouth-wateringly tasty.

May your salads bring good health and happiness to your table!

Salad Vegetables

The salad vegetable is any type of vegetable that earns its keep in a salad by virtue of freshness and flavour. Vegetables for a salad can be raw or lightly cooked. If cooked, they are best served at room temperature to bring out their full flavour. Here is a selection of the most commonly used salad vegetables.

Avocado pear

This has a smooth, buttery flesh when ripe and is an asset to many salads, of which Guacamole is perhaps the best known. Avocados can also be served on their own as a starter, with a light vinaigrette dressing or a spoonful of lemon mayonnaise, or even just a squeeze of lemon juice and salt.

Carrots

These should be young, slender and sweet to taste. Either cooked or raw, they bring flavour and colour to a salad.

Celery

A useful salad vegetable, celery is grown year round for its robust, earthy flavour. The crisp stems should be neither stringy nor tough. Celery partners well with cooked ham, apple and walnut in Waldorf Salad and is also used as a crudité.

Courgettes

These can be bitter to taste and are usually cooked before being combined with other young vegetables. Smooth in texture when cooked, they blend well with tomatoes, aubergines, peppers and onions. Use baby courgettes for a sweeter flavour if you want to serve raw courgettes as a crudité.

Cucumbers

A common salad ingredient that turns up, invited or not, in salad bowls everywhere. The quality of this vegetable is best appreciated in strongly-flavoured salads.

Fennel

The bulb (or Florence) variety has a strong, aniseed flavour and looks like a squat head of celery. Because the flavour can be dominant, it may be blanched in boiling water for 6 minutes before use in a salad.

Garlic

Strong to taste, garlic is essential to the robust cooking of South America, Asia and the Mediterranean. Garlic should be used carefully as it can mask other flavours, but it is a vital part of salad preparation. To impart a very gentle hint of garlic rub round the inside of your salad bowl with a cut clove. Another way to moderate the strength of fresh garlic is to store a few crushed cloves in a bottle of olive oil, and use the oil sparingly in dressings.

Green beans

The varieties are too numerous to mention here, but they all have their merits as salad vegetables. To appreciate the sweet flavour of young tender green beans, cook them for 6 minutes and then refresh immediately in cold running water so that the crispness and colour are retained. An essential ingredient of Salade Niçoise, green beans are an ideal crudité and also partner well with a spicy tomato sauce.

Mushrooms

These provide a rich tone to many salads and are eaten both raw and cooked. The oyster mushroom, which grows wild but is also cultivated, has a fine flavour and texture. White mushrooms are widely available and are often used raw, thinly sliced, in a mixed salad. Chestnut mushrooms are similar to white mushrooms but have slightly more flavour.

Onions

Several varieties are suited to salads. The strongest is the small, brown onion, which should be chopped finely and used sparingly. Less strong is the large, white Spanish onion, which has a sweeter, milder flavour and may be used coarsely chopped.

Potatoes

A staple carbohydrate ingredient to add bulk to a salad or provide a main element.

Spring onions

These have a milder flavour than the common onion and give a gentle bite to many popular salads.

Baby sweetcorn

Baby sweetcorn cobs can be eaten whole, lightly cooked or raw, and should be served warm or at room temperature.

Tomatoes

Technically a fruit rather than a vegetable, tomatoes are valued for their flavour and colour. Dwarf varieties usually ripen more quickly than large ones and have a better flavour.

Salad Fruit

The contents of the fruit bowl offer endless possibilities for sweet and savoury salads.

Apples
This versatile fruit offers a unique flavour to both sweet and savoury salads.

Apricots
Use apricots raw, dried or lightly poached.

Bananas
These bring a special richness to fruit salads, although their flavour can often interfere with more delicate fruit.

Blackberries
With a very short season, wild blackberries have more flavour than cultivated.

Blueberries
These tight-skinned berries combine well with the sharpness of fresh oranges.

Cape gooseberries
Small, fragrant, pleasantly tart orange berries, wrapped in a paper cape.

Cherries
Cherries should be firm and glossy and are a deliciously colourful ingredient in many kinds of fruit salad.

Cranberries
Too sharp to eat raw but very good for cooking.

Dates
Fresh dates are sweet and juicy, dried ones have a more intense flavour. Both kinds work well in fresh fruit salads.

Figs
Green or purple skinned fruit, with sweet, pinkish-red flesh. Eat whole or peeled.

Gooseberries
Dessert types can be eaten raw but cooking varieties are more widely available.

Grapefruit
These can have yellow, green or pink flesh; the pink-fleshed or ruby varieties are the sweetest.

Grapes
Large Muscat varieties, whose season runs from late summer to autumn, are the most coveted and also the most expensive.

Kiwi fruit
Available all the year round.

Kumquats
Tiny relatives of the orange and can be eaten raw or cooked.

Lemons and limes
Both these indispensable citrus fruits are used for flavour, and to prevent fruit turning brown.

Lychees
A small fruit with a hard pink skin and sweet, juicy flesh.

Mangoes
Tropical fruit with an exotic flavour and golden-orange flesh that is wonderful in sweet or savoury salads.

Melons
These grow in abundance from mid to late summer and provide a resource of freshness and flavour. Melon is at its most delicious served icy cold.

Nectarines
A relative of the peach with a smoother skin.

Oranges
At their best during winter, they can be segmented and added to sweet and savoury salads.

Pawpaws
These fruits of the tropics have a distinctive, sweet flavour. When ripe they are yellow–green.

Peaches
Choose white peaches for the sweetest flavour, and yellow for a more aromatic taste.

Pears
Perfect for savoury salads, and with strong blue cheese and toasted pecan nuts.

Pineapples
Ripe pineapples resist firm pressure in the hand and have a sweet smell.

Plums
There are many dessert and cooking varieties.

Raspberries
Much-coveted soft fruits that partner well with ripe mango, passion fruit and strawberries.

Rhubarb
Technically a vegetable, too tart to eat raw.

Star fruit
When sliced, this makes a pretty shape perfect for garnishes.

Strawberries
A popular summer fruit, especially served with cream.

Lettuces and Leaves

One particular aspect of lettuce that sets it apart from any other vegetable is that you can only buy it in one form – fresh.

Lettuce has been cultivated for thousands of years. In Egyptian times it was sacred to the fertility god Min. It was then considered a powerful aphrodisiac, yet for the Greeks and the Romans it was thought to have quite the opposite effect, making one sleepy and generally soporific. Chemists today confirm that lettuce contains a hypnotic similar to opium, and in herbal remedies lettuce is recommended for insomniacs.

There are hundreds of different varieties of lettuce. Today, an increasing choice is available in the shops so that the salad bowl can become a wealth of colour, taste and texture with no other ingredient than a selection of leaves.

Butterhead

These are the classic round lettuces. They have a pale heart and floppy, loosely packed leaves. They have a pleasant flavour as long as they are fresh. Choose the lettuce with the best heart by picking it up at the bottom and gently squeezing to check there is a firm centre.

Lollo Rosso

Lollo rosso and lollo biondo – similar in shape but a paler green without any purple edges – are both non-hearting lettuces. Although they do not have a lot of flavour they look superb and are often used to form a nest of leaves on which to place the rest of a salad.

Cos

The cos lettuce would have been known in antiquity. It has two names, cos, derived from the Greek island where it was found; and romaine, the name used by the French. Cos is considered to have the best flavour and is the correct lettuce for use in Caesar Salad.

Escarole

Escarole is one of the more robust lettuces in terms of flavour and texture. Like the curly-leafed endive, escarole has a distinct bitter flavour. Served with other leaves and a well-flavoured dressing, escarole and endive will give your salad a pleasant "bite".

Oak Leaf Lettuce

Oak leaf lettuce, together with lollo rosso and lollo biondo, is another member of the loosehead lettuce group. Oak leaf lettuce has a very gentle flavour. It is a very decorative leaf and makes a beautiful addition to any salad, and a lovely garnish.

Little Gem

These look like something between a baby cos and a tightly-furled butterhead. They have firm hearts and a distinct flavour. Their tight centres mean that they can be sliced whole and the quarters used for carrying slivers of smoked fish or anchovy as a simple starter.

Chinese Leaves

This has pale green, crinkly leaves with long, wide, white ribs. Its shape is a little like a very fat head of celery, which gives rise to another of its names, celery cabbage. It is crunchy, and since it is available all year round, it makes a useful winter salad component.

Radicchio

This is a variety developed from wild chicory. It looks like a lettuce with deep wine-red leaves and cream ribs and owes its splendid foliage to careful shading from the light. If it is grown in the dark the leaves are marbled pink. Its bitter flavour contrasts well with green salads.

Lamb's Lettuce

Lamb's lettuce or corn salad is a popular winter leaf that does not actually belong to the lettuce family, but is terrific in salads. Called mache in France, lamb's lettuce has small, attractive, dark green leaves and grows in pretty little sprigs. Its flavour is mild and nutty.

Watercress

Watercress is perhaps the most robustly flavoured of all the salad ingredients and a handful of watercress is all you need to perk up a dull salad. It has a distinctive "raw" flavour, peppery and slightly pungent, and this, together with its shiny leaves, make it a popular garnish.

Rocket

Rocket has a wonderful peppery flavour and is excellent in a mixed green salad. It was eaten by the Greeks and Romans as an aphrodisiac. Since it has such a striking flavour a little goes a long way; just a few leaves will transform a green salad and liven up a sandwich.

Herbs

For as long as salads have drawn on the qualities of fresh produce, sweet herbs have played an important part in providing individual character and flavour. When herbs are used in a salad, they should be as full of life as the salad leaves they accompany. Dried herbs are no substitute for fresh ones and should be kept for cooked dishes such as casseroles. Salad herbs are distinguished by their ability to release flavour without lengthy cooking.

Most salad herbs belong finely chopped in salad dressings and marinades, while the robust flavours of rosemary, thyme and fennel branches can be used on the barbecue to impart a smoky herb flavour. Ideally salad herbs should be picked just before use, but if you cannot use them immediately keep them in water to retain their freshness. Parsley, mint and coriander will keep for up to a week in this way if also covered with a plastic bag and placed in the fridge.

Basil

Remarkable for its fresh, pungent flavour unlike that of any other herb, basil is widely used in Mediterranean salads, especially Italian recipes. Basil leaves are tender and delicate and should be gently torn or snipped with scissors, rather than chopped with a knife.

Chives

Chives belong to the onion family and have a mild onion flavour. The slender, green stems and soft mauve flowers are both edible. Chives are an indispensable flavouring for potato salads.

Coriander

The chopped leaves of this pungent, distinctively flavoured herb are popular in Middle Eastern and Eastern salads.

Lavender

This soothingly fragrant herb is edible and may be used in both sweet and savoury salads as it combines well with thyme, garlic, honey and orange.

Mint

This much-loved herb is widely used in Greek and Middle Eastern salads, such as Tzatziki and Tabbouleh. It is also a popular addition to fruit salads. Garden mint is the most common variety; others include spearmint and the round-leafed apple mint.

Above: Clockwise from top left; thyme, coriander, parsley, chives, lavender, rose , mint and basil.

Parsley

Flat- and curly-leaf parsley are both used for their fresh, green flavour. Flat-leaf parsley is said to have a stronger taste. Freshly chopped parsley is used by the handful in salads and dressings.

Rose

Although it is not technically a herb, the sweet-scented rose can be used to flavour fresh fruit salads. It combines well with blackberries and raspberries.

Thyme

An asset to salads featuring rich, earthy flavours, this herb has a penetrating flavour.

Spices

Spices are the aromatic seasonings found in the seed, bark, fruit and sometimes flowers of certain plants and trees. Spices are highly valued for their warm, inviting flavours, and thankfully their price is relatively low. The flavour of a spice is contained in the volatile oils of the seed, bark or fruit; so, like herbs, spices should be used as fresh as possible. Whole spices keep better than ground ones, which tend to lose their freshness in 3–4 months.

Not all spices are suitable for salad making, although many allow us to explore the flavours of other cultures. The recipes in this book use curry spices in moderation so as not to spoil the delicate salad flavours.

Caraway

These savoury-sweet-tasting seeds are widely used in German and Austrian cooking and feature strongly in many Jewish dishes. The small ribbed seeds are similar in appearance and taste to cumin. The flavour combines especially well with German mustard in a dressing for frankfurter salad.

Cayenne pepper

Also known as chilli powder, this is the dried and finely ground fruit of the hot chilli pepper. It is an important seasoning in South American cooking and is often used when seasoning fish and seafood. Cayenne pepper can be blended with paprika if it is too hot and should be used with care.

Celery salt

A combination of ground celery seed and salt, this is used for seasoning vegetables, especially carrots.

Cumin seeds

Often associated with Aisan and North African cookery, cumin can be bought ground or as small, slender seeds. It combines well with coriander seeds.

Curry paste

Prepared curry paste consists of a blend of Indian spices preserved in oil. It may be added to dressings, and is particularly useful in this respect for showing off the sweet qualities of fish and shellfish.

Paprika

This spice is made from a variety of sweet red pepper. It is mild in flavour, and adds colour.

Pepper

Undoubtedly the most popular spice used in the West, pepper features in the cooking of

Above: Flavoursome additions to salads include (clockwise from top left) celery salt, caraway seeds, curry paste, saffron strands, peppercorns and cayenne pepper.

almost every nation. Peppercorns can be white, black, green or red and should always be freshly milled rather than bought already ground.

Saffron

The world's most expensive spice, made from the dried stigma of a crocus, real saffron has a tobacco-rich smell and gives a sweet yellow tint to liquids used for cooking. It can be used in creamy dressings and brings out the richness of fish and seafood dishes. There are many powdered imitations which provide colour without the flavour of the real thing.

Oils, Vinegars and Flavourings

OILS

Oil is the main ingredient of most dressings and provides an important richness to salads. Neutral oils, such as sunflower, safflower or groundnut (peanut), are ideally used as a background for stronger oils. Sesame, walnut and hazelnut oils are the strongest and should be used sparingly. Olive oil is prized for its clarity of flavour and clean richness. The most significant producers of olive oil are Italy, France, Spain and Greece. These and other countries produce two main grades of olive oil: estate-grown extra-virgin olive oil; and semi-fine olive oil, which is of a good, basic standard.

Olive oils

French olive oils are subtly flavoured and provide a well-balanced lightness to dressings.

Greek olive oils are typically strong in character. They are often green with a thick texture and are unsuitable for mayonnaise.

Italian olive oils are noted for their vigorous Mediterranean flavours. Tuscan oils are noted for their well-rounded, spicy flavour. Sicilian oils tend to be lighter in texture, although they are often stronger in flavour.

Spanish olive oils are typically fruity and often have a nutty quality with a slight bitterness.

Nut oils

Hazelnut and walnut oils are valued for their strong, nutty flavour. Tasting richly of the nuts from which they are pressed, both are usually blended with neutral oils for salad dressings.

Seed oils

Groundnut (peanut) oil and sunflower oil are valued for their clean, neutral flavour.

SALAD FLAVOURINGS

Capers

These are the pickled flower buds of a bush native to the Mediterranean. Their strong, sharp flavour is well suited to richly flavoured salads.

Lemon and lime juice

The juice of lemons and limes is used to impart a clean acidity to oil dressings. They should be used in moderation.

Mustard

Mustard has a tendency to bring out the flavour of other ingredients. It acts as an emulsifier in dressings and allows oil and vinegar to merge for a short perod of time. The most popular mustards for use in salads are French, German, English and wholegrain.

Above: Top left to right; Italian virgin olive oil, Spanish olive oil, Italian olive oil, Safflower oil, hazelnut oil, walnut oil, groundnut oil, French olive oil, Italian olive oil, white wine vinegar. Left to right bottom; lemon, olives, limes, capers and mustard.

Olives

Black and green olives belong in salads with a Mediterranean flavour. Black olives are generally sweeter than green ones.

VINEGARS

White wine vinegar

This should be used in moderation to balance the richness of an oil. A good-quality white wine vinegar will serve most purposes.

Balsemic vinegar

Sweeter than other vinegars, only a few drops of balsemic vinegar are necessary to enhance a salad or dressing. It is also a good substitute for lemon juice.

Making Herbed Oils and Vinegars

Many herbed oils and vinegars are available commercially, but you can very easily make your own. Pour the oil or vinegar into a sterilized jar and add your flavouring. Allow to steep for 2 weeks, then strain and decant into an attractive bottle which has also been sterilized properly. Add a seal and an identifying label. Flavoured vinegars should be used within 3 months, and flavoured herbs within 10 days. Fresh herbs should be clean and completely dry before you use them.

TARRAGON VINEGAR

Steep tarragon in cider vinegar, then decant. Insert 2 or 3 long sprigs of tarragon into the bottle.

ROSEMARY VINEGAR

Steep a sprig of fresh rosemary in red wine vinegar, then decant. Pour into a sterlized, dry bottle and add a few long stems of rosemary as decoration.

LEMON AND LIME VINEGAR

Steep strips of lemon and lime rind in white wine vinegar, then decant. Pour into a sterilized, clean bottle and add fresh strips of rind for colour.

RASPBERRY VINEGAR

Pour vinegar into a saucepan with 1 tbsp of pickling spices and heat gently for 5 minutes. Pour the hot mixture over the raspberries in a bowl and then add 2 sprigs of lemon thyme. Cover and leave the mixture to infuse for two days in a cool, dark place. Strain the liquid and pour the flavoured vinegar into a sterilized bottle and seal.

DILL AND LEMON OIL

Steep a handful of fresh dill and a large strip of lemon rind in virgin olive oil, then decant. Use for salads containing fish or seafood.

MEDITERRANEAN HERB OIL

Steep rosemary, thyme and marjoram in virgin olive oil, then decant.

BASIL AND CHILLI OIL

Steep basil and 3 chillies in virgin olive oil, then decant. Add to tomato and mozzarella salads.

WARNING

There is some evidence that oils containing fresh herbs and spices can grow harmful moulds, especially once the bottle has been opened and the contents are not fully covered by the oil. To protect against this, it is recommended that the herbs and spices are removed once their flavour has passed into the oil.

Left: Beautiful and delicious, herbal vinegars make exquisite gifts. From left: Tarragon vinegar, Rosemary vinegar, Raspberry vinegar and Lemon and Lime vinegar.

Fruit Preparation

CITRUS FRUIT

1 To peel, cut a slice from the top and from the base. Set the fruit base down on a work surface.

2 Cut off the peel lengthways in thick strips. Take the coloured rind (zest) and all the white pith (which has a bitter taste). Cut following the curve of the fruit.

1 To remove the thin, coloured rind (zest), use a vegetable peeler to shave off the rind in wide strips, taking none of the white pith. Use these strips whole or cut them into fine shreds with a sharp knife.

2 Alternatively, rub the fruit against the fine holes of a metal grater, turning the fruit so that you take just the coloured rind and not the white pith. Or use a special tool, called a citrus zester, to take fine threads of rind. Finely chop the threads for tiny pieces.

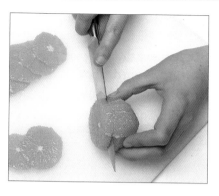

1 For slices, cut across the fruit in slices with a serrated knife.

1 For segments, hold the fruit over a bowl to catch the juice. Working from the side of the fruit to the centre, slide the knife down first one side of a separating membrane and then the other. Continue cutting out segments.

FRESH CURRANTS

1 Pull through the prongs of a fork to remove red, black or white currants from the stalks.

APPLES AND PEARS

1 For whole fruit, use an apple corer to stamp out the whole core from stalk end to base.

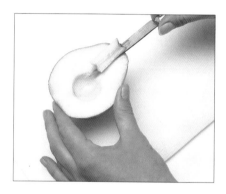

1 For halves, use a melon baller to scoop out the core. Cut out the stalk and base with a sharp knife.

2 For rings, remove the core and seeds. Set the fruit on its side and cut across rings, as required.

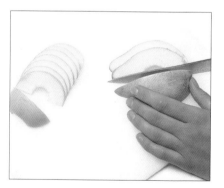

1 For slices, cut the fruit in half and remove the core and seeds. Set one half, cut side down, and cut it across into neat slices. Repeat with the other half.

FRESH DATES

1 Halve the fruit lengthways and lift out the stone.

PAWPAWS AND MELONS

1 Halve the fruit. Scoop out the seeds from the central hollow, then scrape away any fibres. For slices, follow the pear technique.

KIWI FRUIT, STAR FRUIT (CARAMBOLA)

1 Cut the fruit across into neat slices; discard the ends.

PINEAPPLES

1 To peel the pineapple, set the pineapple on its base, hold it at the top and cut thick slices of skin from top to bottom. Dig out any eyes that remain with the point of the knife.

2 For chunks, halve the peeled fruit lengthways and then cut into quarters. Cut each quarter into spears and cut out the core. Cut each spear into chunks.

3 For rings, cut the peeled fruit across into slices and cut out the core.

KEEPING FRESH COLOUR

If exposed to the air for long, the cut flesh of fruits such as apples, bananas and avocados starts to turn brown. So if cut fruit has to wait before being served, sprinkle the cut surfaces with lemon juice, or immerse hard fruits in water and lemon juice, but do not soak or the fruit may become soggy.

MANGOES

1 Cut lengthways on either side of the stone. Then cut from the two thin ends of the stone.

2 Remove the skin and cut the flesh into slices or cubes.

PEACHES, NECTARINES, APRICOTS AND PLUMS

1 Cut the fruit in half, cutting around the indentation. Twist the halves apart. Lift out the stone, or lever it out with the tip of a knife. Or cut the unpeeled fruit into wedges, removing the stone. Set each wedge peel side down and slide the knife down to peel.

BASIL AND LEMON MAYONNAISE

This luxurious dressing is flavoured with lemon juice and two types of basil. Serve with all kinds of leafy salads, crudités or coleslaws. It is also good with baked potatoes or as a delicious dip for French fries. The dressing will keep in an airtight jar for up to a week in the fridge.

INGREDIENTS

Makes about 300 ml/¹/₂ pint/1¹/₄ cups

2 large egg yolks

15 ml/1 tbsp lemon juice

150 ml/¹/₄ pint/²/₃ cup extra-virgin
   olive oil

150 ml/¹/₄ pint/²/₃ cup sunflower oil

4 garlic cloves

handful of fresh green basil

handful of fresh opal basil

salt and ground black pepper

1 Place the egg yolks and lemon juice in a blender or food processor and mix them briefly until lightly blended.

2 In a jug, stir together both oils. With the machine running, pour in the oil very slowly, a little at a time.

3 Once half of the oil has been added, and the dressing has successfully emulsified, the remaining oil can be incorporated more quickly. Continue processing until a thick, creamy mayonnaise has formed.

4 Peel and crush the garlic cloves and add to the mayonnaise. Alternatively, place the cloves on a chopping board and sprinkle with salt, then flatten them with the heel of a heavy-bladed knife and chop the flesh. Flatten the garlic again to make a coarse purée. Add to the mayonnaise.

5 Remove the basil stalks and tear both types of leaves into small pieces. Stir into the mayonnaise.

6 Add salt and pepper to taste, then transfer the mayonnaise to a serving dish. Cover and chill until ready to serve.

Instant Dressings and Dips

If you need an instant dressing or dip, try one of these quick and easy recipes. Most of them use store-cupboard ingredients.

CREAMY BLACK OLIVE DIP

Stir a little black olive paste into a carton of extra-thick double cream until smooth and well blended. Add salt, ground black pepper and a squeeze of lemon juice to taste. Serve chilled.

CRÈME FRAÎCHE DRESSING WITH SPRING ONIONS

Finely chop a bunch of spring onions and stir into a carton of crème fraîche. Add a dash of chilli sauce, a squeeze of lime juice, and salt and ground black pepper.

GREEK-STYLE YOGURT AND MUSTARD DIP

Mix a small carton of creamy, Greek-style yogurt with 5–10 ml/1–2 tsp wholegrain mustard. Serve with crudités.

HERB MAYONNAISE

Liven up ready-made French-style mayonnaise with a handful of chopped fresh herbs – try flat-leaf parsley, basil, dill or tarragon.

PASSATA AND HORSERADISH DIP

Bring a little tang to a small carton or bottle of passata (sieved tomatoes) by adding some horseradish sauce or 5–10 ml/1–2 tsp creamed horseradish and salt and pepper to taste. Serve with lightly-cooked vegetables.

PESTO DIP

For a simple, speedy, Italian-style dip, stir 15 ml/1 tbsp ready-made red or green pesto into a carton of soured cream. Serve with crisp crudités or wedges of oven-roasted Mediterranean vegetables, such as peppers, courgettes and onions, for a delicious starter.

SOFT CHEESE AND CHIVE DIP

Mix a tub of soft cheese with 30–45 ml/2–3 tbsp snipped fresh chives and season to taste with salt and black pepper. If the dip is too thick, stir in a little milk to soften it. Use as a dressing for all kinds of salads, especially winter coleslaws.

Above: Top row; creamy black olive dip, creme fraîche dressing with spring onions. Second row; herb mayonnaise, yogurt and sun-dried tomato dip. Third row; greek-style yogurt and mustard dip, soft cheese and chive dip, spiced yogurt dressing. Fourth row; pesto dip, passata and horseradish dip.

SPICED YOGURT DRESSING

Stir a little curry paste and chutney into a carton of yogurt.

SUN-DRIED TOMATO DIP

Stir 15–30 ml/1–2 tbsp sun-dried tomato paste into a carton of Greek-style yogurt. Season to taste with salt and ground black pepper.

LIGHT & SIDE SALADS

Crudités

A colourful selection of raw vegetables, or crudités, may be served with drinks or as small salad starters. The term "crudités" is used both for small pieces of vegetables served with a tasty dip and for a selection of vegetable salads presented in separate dishes. By choosing contrasting colours, it is possible to make a beautiful presentation of any combination of vegetables, raw or lightly cooked, attractively arranged on a platter or in baskets and served with a tangy dip, such as aïoli (garlic mayonnaise) or tapenade (olive paste). Allow 75–115 g/3–4 oz of each vegetable per person.

AÏOLI

Put four crushed garlic cloves (or more or less, to taste) in a small bowl with a pinch of salt and crush with the back of a spoon. Add two egg yolks and beat for 30 seconds with an electric mixer until creamy. Beat in 250 ml/8 fl oz/1 cup extra-virgin olive oil, by drops, until the mixture thickens. As it begins to thicken, the oil can be added in a thin stream until the mixture is thick. Thin the sauce with a little lemon juice and season to taste. Chill for up to 2 days; bring to room temperature and stir before serving.

TAPENADE

Put 200 g/7 oz pitted black olives, 6 canned anchovy fillets, 30 ml/2 tbsp capers, rinsed, 1–2 garlic cloves, 5 ml/1 tsp fresh thyme leaves, 15 ml/1 tbsp Dijon mustard, the juice of ½ lemon, ground black pepper and, if you like, 15 ml/1 tbsp brandy in a food processor fitted with the metal blade. Process for 15–30 seconds until smooth, then scrape down the sides of the bowl. With the machine running, slowly add 60–90 ml/4–6 tbsp extra-virgin olive oil to make a smooth, firm paste. Store in an airtight container.

RAW VEGETABLE PLATTER

INGREDIENTS

Serves 6–8

2 red and 2 yellow peppers, seeded and sliced lengthways
225 g/8 oz fresh baby corn cobs, blanched
1 chicory head (red or white), trimmed and leaves separated
175–225 g/6–8 oz thin asparagus, trimmed and blanched
1 small bunch radishes with small leaves
175 g/6 oz cherry tomatoes
12 quails' eggs, boiled for 3 minutes, drained, refreshed and peeled
aïoli or tapenade, to serve

Arrange the prepared vegetables on a serving plate together with the quails' eggs. Cover with a damp tea towel until ready to serve. Serve with aïoli or tapenade for dipping.

TOMATO AND CUCUMBER SALAD

INGREDIENTS

Serves 4–6

1 medium cucumber, peeled and thinly sliced
5-6 ice cubes
30 ml/2 tbsp white wine vinegar
90 ml/6 tbsp crème fraîche or soured cream
30 ml/2 tbsp chopped fresh mint
4 or 5 ripe tomatoes, sliced
salt and ground black pepper

Place the cucumber in a bowl, sprinkle with a little salt and 15 ml/1 tbsp of the vinegar and toss with the ice cubes. Chill for 1 hour to crisp, then rinse, drain and pat dry. Return to the bowl, add the cream, pepper and mint and stir to mix well. Arrange the tomato slices on a serving plate, sprinkle with the remaining vinegar and spoon the cucumber slices into the centre.

CARROT AND PARSLEY SALAD

INGREDIENTS

Serves 4–6

1 garlic clove, crushed
grated rind and juice of 1 unwaxed orange
30–45 ml/2–3 tbsp groundnut oil
450 g/1 lb carrots, cut into very fine julienne strips
30–45 ml/2–3 tbsp chopped fresh parsley
salt and ground black pepper

Rub a bowl with the garlic and leave in the bowl. Add the orange rind and juice and salt and pepper. Whisk in the oil until blended, then remove the garlic. Add the carrots and half of the parsley and toss well. Garnish with the remaining parsley.

Lettuce and Herb Salad

Shops now sell many different types of lettuce leaves all year, so try to use a mixture. Look out for pre-packed bags of mixed baby lettuce leaves.

INGREDIENTS

Serves 4

¹/₂ cucumber

mixed lettuce leaves

1 bunch watercress, about 115 g/4 oz

1 chicory head, sliced

45 ml/3 tbsp chopped fresh herbs such as
   parsley, thyme, tarragon, chives, chervil

For the dressing

15 ml/1 tbsp white wine vinegar

5 ml/1 tsp prepared mustard

75 ml/5 tbsp olive oil

salt and ground black pepper

3 Either toss the cucumber, lettuce, watercress, chicory and herbs together in a bowl, or arrange them in the bowl in layers.

4 Stir the dressing, then pour over the salad and toss lightly to coat the salad vegetables and leaves. Serve at once.

1 To make the dressing, mix the vinegar and mustard together, then whisk in the oil and seasoning.

2 Peel the cucumber, if liked, then halve it lengthways and scoop out the seeds. Thinly slice the flesh. Tear the lettuce leaves into bite-size pieces.

Minted Melon and Grapefruit Cocktail

Melon is always a popular starter. Here the flavour is complemented by the refreshing taste of citrus fruit and a simple dressing.

INGREDIENTS

Serves 4

1 small Galia melon, about 1 kg/2¼ lb

2 pink grapefruit

1 yellow grapefruit

5 ml/1 tsp Dijon mustard

5 ml/1 tsp raspberry or sherry vinegar

5 ml/1 tsp clear honey

15 ml/1 tbsp chopped fresh mint

fresh mint sprigs, to garnish

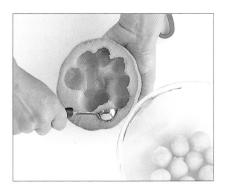

1 Halve the melon and remove the seeds with a teaspoon. With a melon baller, carefully scoop the flesh into balls.

2 With a sharp knife, peel all three grapefruit and cut away all the white pith. Remove the segments by cutting between the membranes, holding the fruit over a bowl to catch any juice.

3 Whisk the mustard, vinegar, honey, chopped mint and grapefruit juice together in a mixing bowl. Add the melon balls and grapefruit segments and mix well. Chill for 30 minutes.

4 Ladle into four serving dishes, garnish each one with a sprig of fresh mint and serve.

Black and Orange Salad

This dramatically colourful salad, with its spicy dressing, is very unusual. It is a feast for the eyes as well as for the taste buds.

INGREDIENTS

Serves 4

3 oranges

115 g/4 oz/1 cup pitted black olives

15 ml/1 tbsp chopped fresh coriander

15 ml/1 tbsp chopped fresh parsley

For the dressing

30 ml/2 tbsp olive oil

15 ml/1 tbsp lemon juice

2.5 ml/½ tsp paprika

2.5 ml/½ tsp ground cumin

1 With a sharp knife, cut away the peel and pith from the oranges and divide the fruit into segments.

2 Place the oranges in a salad bowl and add the black olives, coriander and parsley.

3 Blend together the olive oil, lemon juice, paprika and cumin. Pour the dressing over the salad and toss gently. Chill for about 30 minutes and serve.

Rocket and Coriander Salad

Rocket leaves have a wonderful, peppery flavour. However, unless you have a plentiful supply of rocket, you may well have to use extra spinach or another green leaf to pad out this salad.

INGREDIENTS

Serves 4

115 g/4 oz or more rocket leaves

115 g/4 oz young spinach leaves

1 large bunch fresh coriander, about
    25 g/1 oz

2–3 fresh parsley sprigs

For the dressing

1 garlic clove, crushed

45 ml/3 tbsp olive oil

10 ml/2 tsp white wine vinegar

pinch of paprika

cayenne pepper

salt

1 Place the rocket and spinach leaves in a salad bowl. Chop the coriander and parsley and scatter them over the top.

2 In a small jug, blend together the garlic, olive oil, vinegar, paprika, cayenne pepper and salt.

3 Pour the dressing over the salad and serve immediately.

Caesar Salad

There are many stories about the origin of Caesar Salad. The most likely is that it was invented by an Italian, Caesar Cardini, who owned a restaurant in Mexico in the 1920s. Simplicity is the key to the success of this salad.

INGREDIENTS

Serves 4

3 slices day-old bread, 1 cm/½ in thick

60 ml/4 tbsp garlic oil

50 g/2 oz piece Parmesan cheese

1 cos lettuce

salt and ground black pepper

For the dressing

2 egg yolks, as fresh as possible

25 g/1 oz canned anchovy fillets, drained and roughly chopped

2.5 ml/½ tsp French mustard

120 ml/4 fl oz/½ cup olive oil

15 ml/1 tbsp white wine vinegar

1 To make the dressing, combine the egg yolks, anchovies, mustard, oil and vinegar in a screw-top jar and shake well.

2 Remove the crusts from the bread with a serrated knife and cut into 2.5 cm/1 in fingers.

3 Heat the garlic oil in a large frying-pan, add the pieces of bread and fry until golden. Sprinkle with salt and leave to drain on kitchen paper.

4 Cut thin shavings from the Parmesan cheese with a vegetable peeler.

5 Wash the lettuce leaves and spin dry. Smother with the dressing, and scatter with the garlic croûtons and Parmesan cheese shavings. Season and serve.

COOK'S TIP

The classic dressing for Caesar Salad is made with raw egg yolks. Ensure that you use only the freshest eggs, bought from a reputable supplier. Expectant mothers, young children and the elderly are not advised to eat raw egg yolks. You could omit them from the dressing and grate hard-boiled yolks on top of the salad instead.

Turkish Salad

This classic salad is a wonderful combination of textures and flavours. The saltiness of the cheese is perfectly balanced by the refreshing salad vegetables.

INGREDIENTS

Serves 4

1 cos lettuce heart

1 green pepper

1 red pepper

½ cucumber

4 tomatoes

1 red onion

225 g/8 oz/2 cups feta cheese, crumbled

black olives, to garnish

For the dressing

45 ml/3 tbsp olive oil

45 ml/3 tbsp lemon juice

1 garlic clove, crushed

15 ml/1 tbsp chopped fresh parsley

15 ml/1 tbsp chopped fresh mint

salt and ground black pepper

1 Chop the lettuce into bite-size pieces. Seed the peppers, remove the cores and cut the flesh into thin strips. Chop the cucumber and slice or chop the tomatoes. Cut the onion in half, then slice finely.

2 Place the chopped lettuce, peppers, cucumber, tomatoes and onion in a large bowl. Scatter the feta over the top and toss together lightly.

3 To make the dressing, blend together the olive oil, lemon juice and garlic in a small bowl. Stir in the chopped parsley and mint and season with salt and pepper to taste.

4 Pour the dressing over the salad and toss lightly. Garnish with a handful of black olives and serve immediately.

Persian Salad

This very simple salad can be served with almost any dish. Don't add the dressing until just before you are ready to serve.

INGREDIENTS

Serves 4

4 tomatoes

½ cucumber

1 onion

1 cos lettuce heart

For the dressing

30 ml/2 tbsp olive oil

juice of 1 lemon

1 garlic clove, crushed

salt and ground black pepper

1 Cut the tomatoes and cucumber into small cubes. Finely chop the onion and tear the lettuce into pieces.

2 Place the prepared tomatoes, cucumber, onion and lettuce in a large salad bowl and mix lightly together.

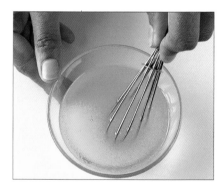

3 To make the dressing, pour the olive oil into a small bowl. Add the lemon juice, garlic and seasoning and blend together well.

4 Pour over the salad and toss lightly to mix. Sprinkle with extra black pepper and serve.

Spinach and Mushroom Salad

This nutritious salad goes well with strongly flavoured dishes. If served alone as a light lunch, it could be dressed with a French vinaigrette and served with warm, crusty French bread.

INGREDIENTS

Serves 4

10 baby corn cobs

2 medium tomatoes

115 g/4 oz/1½ cups mushrooms

1 medium onion cut into rings

20 small spinach leaves

25 g/1 oz salad cress (optional)

salt and ground black pepper

1 Halve the baby corn cobs lengthways and slice the tomatoes.

2 Trim the mushrooms and cut them into thin slices.

3 Arrange all the salad ingredients attractively in a large bowl. Season with salt and pepper and serve.

Nutty Salad

A delicious salad with a tangy bite to it which can be served as an accompaniment to a main meal, or as an appetizer. For wholesome finger food at a party, serve mini pitta breads stuffed with the salad.

INGREDIENTS

Serves 4

1 medium onion, cut into 12 rings

115 g/4 oz/¾ cup canned red kidney beans, drained

1 medium green courgette, sliced

1 medium yellow courgette, sliced

50 g/2 oz pasta shells, cooked

50 g/2 oz/½ cup cashew nuts

25 g/1 oz/¼ cup peanuts

lime wedges and fresh coriander sprigs, to garnish

For the dressing

120 ml/4 fl oz/½ cup fromage frais

30 ml/2 tbsp plain yogurt

1 green chilli, chopped

15 ml/1 tbsp chopped fresh coriander

2.5 ml/½ tsp crushed black peppercorns

2.5 ml/½ tsp crushed dried red chillies

15 ml/1 tbsp lemon juice

2.5 ml/½ tsp salt

1 Arrange the onion rings, red kidney beans, green and yellow courgette slices and pasta shells in a salad dish, ready for serving. Sprinkle the cashew nuts and peanuts over the top.

2 In a separate bowl, blend together the fromage frais, yogurt, green chilli, coriander and salt and beat well using a fork.

3 Sprinkle the crushed black pepper, red chillies and lemon juice over the dressing. Garnish the salad with the lime wedges and coriander sprigs and serve with the dressing in a separate bowl or poured over the salad.

Fresh Ceps Salad

To capture the just-picked flavour of a cep, this delicious salad is enriched with an egg yolk and walnut oil dressing. Choose small ceps which will have a firm texture and the very best flavour.

INGREDIENTS

Serves 4

350 g/12 oz fresh ceps

175 g/6 oz mixed salad leaves, including batavia, young spinach and frisée

50 g/2 oz/½ cup broken walnut pieces, toasted

50 g/2 oz piece Parmesan cheese

salt and ground black pepper

For the dressing

2 egg yolks

2.5 ml/½ tsp French mustard

75 ml/5 tbsp groundnut oil

45 ml/3 tbsp walnut oil

30 ml/2 tbsp lemon juice

30 ml/2 tbsp chopped fresh parsley

pinch of caster sugar

1 To make the dressing, place the egg yolks in a screw-top jar with the mustard, groundnut and walnut oils, lemon juice, parsley and sugar. Shake well.

2 Trim the ceps and cut them into thin slices.

3 Place the ceps in a large salad bowl and combine with the dressing. Leave for 10–15 minutes for the flavours to mingle.

4 Wash and dry the salad leaves, then toss them together with the ceps.

5 Turn the ceps out on to four large serving plates. Season well, scatter with the toasted walnuts and shavings of Parmesan cheese, then serve.

Classic Greek Salad

If you have ever visited Greece, you'll know that this salad accompanied by a chunk of bread makes a delicious first course.

INGREDIENTS

Serves 4

1 cos lettuce

½ cucumber, halved lengthways

4 tomatoes

8 spring onions, sliced

black olives

115 g/4 oz feta cheese

For the dressing

90 ml/6 tbsp white wine vinegar

150 ml/¼ pint/⅔ cup extra-virgin
    olive oil

salt and ground black pepper

1 Tear the lettuce leaves into pieces and place in a large bowl. Slice the cucumber and add to the bowl.

2 Cut the tomatoes into wedges and put them into the bowl.

COOK'S TIP

The salad can be assembled in advance and chilled, but should be dressed only just before serving. Keep the dressing at room temperature as chilling deadens the flavour.

3 Add the spring onions to the bowl together with the olives, and toss well.

4 Cut the feta cheese into cubes and add to the salad.

5 Put the vinegar, olive oil and seasoning into a small bowl and whisk well. Pour the dressing over the salad and toss to combine. Serve at once, with extra olives and chunks of bread, if liked.

Orange and Red Onion Salad with Cumin

Cumin and mint give this refreshing salad a very Middle Eastern flavour. Small, seedless oranges are most suitable, if available.

INGREDIENTS

Serves 6

6 oranges

2 red onions

15 ml/1 tbsp cumin seeds

5 ml/1 tsp coarsely ground black pepper

15 ml/1 tbsp chopped fresh mint

90 ml/6 tbsp olive oil

salt

fresh mint sprigs and black olives, to serve

1 Slice the oranges thinly, working over a bowl to catch any juice. Then, holding each orange slice in turn over the bowl, cut round with scissors to remove the peel and pith. Reserve the juice. Slice the onions thinly and separate into rings.

2 Arrange the orange and onion slices in layers in a shallow dish, sprinkling each layer with cumin seeds, black pepper, chopped mint, olive oil and salt to taste. Pour over the reserved orange juice.

3 Leave the salad to marinate in a cool place for about 2 hours. Scatter over the mint sprigs and black olives, and serve.

Spanish Salad with Capers and Olives

Make this refreshing salad in the summer when tomatoes are at their sweetest and full of flavour.

INGREDIENTS

Serves 4

4 tomatoes

½ cucumber

1 bunch spring onions, trimmed and chopped

1 bunch watercress

8 stuffed olives

30 ml/2 tbsp drained capers

For the dressing

30 ml/2 tbsp red wine vinegar

5 ml/1 tsp paprika

2.5 ml/½ tsp ground cumin

1 garlic clove, crushed

75 ml/5 tbsp olive oil

salt and ground black pepper

1 Peel the tomatoes and finely dice the flesh. Put them in a salad bowl.

2 Peel the cucumber, dice it finely and add it to the tomatoes. Add half the spring onions to the salad bowl and mix lightly. Break the watercress into sprigs. Add to the tomato mixture, with the olives and capers.

3 To make the dressing, mix the wine vinegar, paprika, cumin and garlic in a bowl. Whisk in the oil and add salt and pepper to taste. Pour over the salad and toss lightly. Serve immediately with the remaining spring onions.

Carrot and Orange Salad

A fruit and a vegetable that could have been made for each other form the basis of this wonderful, fresh-tasting salad.

INGREDIENTS

Serves 4

450 g/1 lb carrots

2 large oranges

15 ml/1 tbsp olive oil

30 ml/2 tbsp lemon juice

pinch of sugar (optional)

30 ml/2 tbsp chopped pistachio nuts or toasted pine nuts

salt and ground black pepper

1 Peel the carrots and grate them into a large bowl.

2 Peel the oranges with a sharp knife and cut into segments, catching the juice in a small bowl.

3 Blend together the olive oil, lemon juice and orange juice. Season with a little salt and pepper to taste, and sugar if liked.

4 Toss the orange segments together with the carrots and pour the dressing over. Scatter the salad with the pistachio nuts or pine nuts before serving.

Spinach and Roast Garlic Salad

Don't worry about the amount of garlic in this salad. During roasting, the garlic becomes sweet and subtle and loses its pungent taste.

INGREDIENTS

Serves 4

12 garlic cloves, unpeeled

60 ml/4 tbsp extra-virgin olive oil

450 g/1 lb baby spinach leaves

50 g/2 oz/½ cup pine nuts, lightly toasted

juice of ½ lemon

salt and ground black pepper

1 Preheat the oven to 190°C/ 375°F/Gas 5. Place the garlic in a small roasting tin, toss in 30 ml/ 2 tbsp of the olive oil and roast for about 15 minutes, until the garlic cloves are slightly charred around the edges.

2 While still warm, tip the garlic into a salad bowl. Add the spinach, pine nuts, lemon juice, remaining olive oil and a little salt. Toss well and add black pepper to taste. Serve immediately, inviting guests to squeeze the softened garlic purée out of the skin to eat.

Mixed Green Salad

A good combination of leaves for this salad would be rocket, radicchio, lamb's lettuce and curly endive, with herbs such as chervil, basil, parsley and tarragon.

INGREDIENTS

Serves 4–6

1 garlic clove, peeled

30 ml/2 tbsp red wine or sherry vinegar

5 ml/1 tsp Dijon mustard (optional)

75–120 ml/5–8 tbsp extra-virgin olive oil

200–225 g/7–8 oz mixed salad leaves
    and herbs

salt and ground black pepper

1 Rub a large salad bowl with the garlic clove. Leave the garlic clove in the bowl.

2 Add the vinegar, salt and pepper and mustard, if using. Stir to mix the ingredients and dissolve the salt, then whisk in the olive oil slowly.

3 Remove the garlic clove and stir the vinaigrette to combine.

4 Add the salad leaves to the bowl and toss well. Serve the salad at once before it starts to wilt.

VARIATION

A salad like this should always contain some pungent leaves. Try young dandelion leaves when they are in season, but be sure to pick them well away from traffic routes and agricultural crop spraying.

Apple and Celeriac Salad

Celeriac, despite its coarse appearance, has a sweet and subtle flavour. Traditionally par-boiled in lemony water, in this salad it is served raw, allowing its unique taste and texture to come through.

INGREDIENTS

Serves 3–4

675 g/1½ lb celeriac, peeled

10–15 ml/2–3 tsp lemon juice

5 ml/1 tsp walnut oil (optional)

1 apple

45 ml/3 tbsp mayonnaise

10 ml/2 tsp Dijon mustard

15 ml/1 tbsp chopped fresh parsley

salt and ground black pepper

1 Using a food processor or coarse cheese grater, shred the celeriac. Alternatively, cut it into very thin julienne strips.

2 Place the prepared celeriac in a bowl and sprinkle with the lemon juice and the walnut oil, if using. Stir well to mix.

3 Peel the apple if desired. Cut the apple into quarters and remove the core. Slice the apple quarters thinly crossways and toss together with the celeriac.

4 Mix together the mayonnaise, mustard, parsley and salt and pepper to taste. Add to the celeriac mixture and stir well. Chill for several hours until ready to serve.

Chicory, Fruit and Nut Salad

The mildly bitter taste of the attractive white chicory leaves combines wonderfully well with sweet fruit, and is especially delicious when complemented by a creamy curry sauce.

INGREDIENTS

Serves 4

45 ml/3 tbsp mayonnaise

15 ml/1 tbsp Greek yogurt

15 ml/1 tbsp mild curry paste

90 ml/6 tbsp single cream

½ iceberg lettuce

2 chicory heads

50 g/2 oz/½ cup cashew nuts

50 g/2 oz/1¼ cups flaked coconut

2 red apples

75 g/3 oz/⅓ cup currants

1 Mix the mayonnaise, yogurt, curry paste and single cream in a small bowl. Cover and chill until required.

2 Tear the lettuce into pieces and put into a mixing bowl.

3 Cut the root end off each head of chicory, separate the leaves and add them to the lettuce. Preheat the grill.

4 Grill the cashew nuts for 2 minutes, until golden. Tip into a bowl and set aside. Spread out the coconut on a baking sheet. Grill for 1 minute, until golden.

5 Quarter the apples and cut out the cores. Slice the apples and add them to the lettuce with the toasted coconut and cashew nuts and the currants.

6 Spoon the dressing over the salad, toss lightly and serve.

COOK'S TIP

Watch the coconut flakes and cashew nuts with great care when they are under the grill, as they brown very fast.

Fennel, Orange and Rocket Salad

This light and refreshing salad is an ideal accompaniment to serve with spicy or rich foods.

INGREDIENTS

Serves 4

2 oranges

1 fennel bulb

115 g/4 oz rocket leaves

50 g/2 oz/⅓ cup black olives

For the dressing

30 ml/2 tbsp extra-virgin olive oil

15 ml/1 tbsp balsamic vinegar

1 small garlic clove, crushed

salt and ground black pepper

1 With a vegetable peeler, cut thin strips of rind from the oranges, leaving the pith behind. Cut the rind into thin julienne strips. Cook in boiling water for a few minutes, then drain.

2 Peel the oranges, removing all the white pith. Slice them into thin rounds and discard any seeds.

3 Cut the fennel bulb in half lengthways. Slice across the bulb as thinly as possible, using a food processor fitted with a slicing disc. Alternatively you can use a mandoline.

4 Combine the oranges and fennel in a serving bowl and toss with the rocket leaves.

5 Mix together the oil, vinegar, garlic and seasoning. Pour over the salad, toss together well and leave to stand for a few minutes. Sprinkle with the black olives and the julienne strips of orange and serve.

Aubergine, Lemon and Caper Salad

This cooked vegetable relish is delicious served as an accompaniment to cold meats, with pasta, or simply on its own with some good, crusty bread. Make sure the aubergine is well cooked until it is meltingly soft.

INGREDIENTS

Serves 4

1 large aubergine, about 675 g/1½ lb

60 ml/4 tbsp olive oil

grated rind and juice of 1 lemon

30 ml/2 tbsp capers, rinsed

12 pitted green olives

30 ml/2 tbsp chopped fresh
    flat-leaf parsley

salt and ground black pepper

1 Cut the aubergine into 2.5 cm/ 1 in cubes. Heat the olive oil in a large frying pan and cook the aubergine cubes over a medium heat for about 10 minutes, tossing regularly, until golden and softened. You may need to do this in two batches. Drain on kitchen paper and sprinkle with a little salt.

2 Place the aubergine cubes in a large serving bowl. Toss with the lemon rind and juice, capers, olives and chopped parsley, and season well with salt and pepper. Serve at room temperature.

COOK'S TIP

This will taste even better when made the day before. It will store, covered, in the fridge, for up to 4 days.

Apple Coleslaw

The term coleslaw stems from the Dutch koolsla, meaning "cool cabbage". There are many variations of this salad; this recipe combines the sweet flavours of apple and carrot with celery salt. Coleslaw is traditionally served with cold ham.

INGREDIENTS

Serves 4

450 g/1 lb white cabbage

1 medium onion

2 apples, peeled and cored

175 g/6 oz carrots, peeled

150 ml/¼ pint/⅔ cup mayonnaise

5 ml/1 tsp celery salt

ground black pepper

1 Discard the outside leaves of the white cabbage if they are dirty, cut the cabbage into 5 cm/ 2 in wedges, then remove the stem section.

2 Feed the cabbage and the onion through a food processor fitted with a slicing blade. Change to a grating blade and grate the apples and carrots. Alternatively use a hand grater and vegetable slicer.

3 Combine all the salad ingredients in a large serving bowl. Fold in the mayonnaise and season with the celery salt and black pepper.

VARIATION

For a richer coleslaw, add 115 g/ 4 oz/½ cup grated Cheddar cheese. You may find you will need smaller portions, as the cheese makes a more filling dish.

Carrot, Raisin and Apricot Coleslaw

A tasty variation on classic coleslaw, this colourful salad combines cabbage, carrots and two kinds of dried fruit in a yogurt dressing.

INGREDIENTS

Serves 6

350 g/12 oz/3 cups white cabbage, finely shredded

225 g/8 oz/1½ cups carrots, grated

1 red onion, finely sliced

3 celery sticks, sliced

175 g/6 oz/generous 1 cup raisins

75 g/3 oz/¾ cup dried apricots, chopped

For the dressing

120 ml/4 fl oz/½ cup mayonnaise

90 ml/6 tbsp plain yogurt

30 ml/2 tbsp chopped fresh mixed herbs

salt and ground black pepper

1 Put the cabbage and carrots in a large bowl.

2 Add the onion, celery, raisins and apricots and mix well.

3 In a small bowl, mix together the mayonnaise, yogurt, herbs and seasoning.

4 Add the mayonnaise dressing to the coleslaw ingredients and toss together to mix. Cover and chill for before serving.

VARIATION

Use other dried fruit such as sultanas and ready-to-eat dried pears or peaches in place of the raisins and apricots.

Tzatziki

Tzatziki is a Greek cucumber salad dressed with yogurt, mint and garlic. It is typically served with grilled lamb and chicken, but is also good with salmon and trout.

INGREDIENTS

Serves 4

1 cucumber

5 ml/1 tsp salt

45 ml/3 tbsp finely chopped fresh mint, plus a few sprigs to garnish

1 garlic clove, crushed

5 ml/1 tsp caster sugar

200 ml/7 fl oz/scant 1 cup Greek yogurt

paprika, to garnish (optional)

1 Peel the cucumber. Reserve a little to use as a garnish if you wish and cut the rest in half, lengthways. Remove the seeds with a teaspoon and discard. Slice the cucumber thinly and combine with the salt. Leave for approximately 15–20 minutes. The salt will soften the cucumber and draw out any bitter juices.

2 Place the chopped mint, garlic, sugar and yogurt in a bowl. Stir well to combine.

3 Rinse the cucumber in a sieve under cold running water to flush away the salt. Drain well and combine with the yogurt mixture in a serving bowl. Decorate with sprigs of mint. Garnish with paprika, if you wish.

COOK'S TIP

If preparing tzatziki in a hurry, do not salt the cucumber. The cucumber will have a more crunchy texture, and will be slightly less sweet.

Marinated Cucumber Salad

A wonderfully cooling salad for the summer, with the distinctive flavour of fresh dill.

INGREDIENTS

Serves 4–6

2 medium cucumbers
15 ml/1 tbsp salt
90 g/3½ oz/½ cup granulated sugar
175 ml/6 fl oz/¾ cup dry cider
15 ml/1 tbsp cider vinegar
45 ml/3 tbsp chopped fresh dill
ground black pepper

1 Slice the cucumbers thinly and place them in a colander, sprinkling salt between each layer. Put the colander over a bowl and leave to drain for 1 hour.

2 Thoroughly rinse the cucumber under cold running water to remove excess salt, then pat dry with kitchen paper.

3 Gently heat the sugar, cider and vinegar in a saucepan, until the sugar has dissolved. Remove from the heat and leave to cool. Put the cucumber slices in a bowl, pour over the cider mixture and leave to marinate for 2 hours.

4 Drain the cucumber and sprinkle with the dill and pepper to taste. Mix well and transfer to a serving dish. Chill until ready to serve.

COOK'S TIP

The salad would be a perfect accompaniment for fresh salmon.

Flower Garden Salad

Dress a colourful mixture of salad leaves with good olive oil and freshly squeezed lemon juice, then top it with crispy bread crostini.

INGREDIENTS

Serves 4–6

3 thick slices day-old bread, such as
    ciabatta

120 ml/4 fl oz/½ cup extra-virgin olive oil

1 garlic clove, halved

½ small cos lettuce

½ small oak-leaf lettuce

25 g/1 oz rocket leaves or salad cress

25 g/1 oz fresh flat-leaf parsley

a small handful of young dandelion leaves

juice of 1 lemon

a few nasturtium leaves and flowers

pansy and pot marigold flowers

sea salt flakes and ground black pepper

1 Cut the slices of bread into 1 cm/½ in cubes.

2 Heat half the oil gently in a frying pan and fry the bread cubes in it, tossing them until they are well coated and lightly browned. Remove and cool.

3 Rub the inside of a large salad bowl with the cut sides of the garlic clove, then discard. Pour the remaining oil into the bottom of the bowl.

4 Tear all the salad leaves into bite-size pieces and pile them into the bowl with the oil. Season with salt and pepper. Cover and keep chilled until you are ready to serve the salad.

5 To serve, toss the leaves in the oil at the bottom of the bowl, then sprinkle with the lemon juice and toss again. Scatter the crostini and the flowers over the top and serve immediately.

Fresh Spinach and Avocado Salad

Young, tender spinach leaves make a change from lettuce. They are delicious served with avocado, cherry tomatoes and radishes in an unusual tofu sauce.

INGREDIENTS

Serves 2–3

1 large avocado
juice of 1 lime
225 g/8 oz baby spinach leaves
115 g/4 oz cherry tomatoes
4 spring onions, sliced
½ cucumber
50 g/2 oz radishes, sliced

For the dressing

115 g/4 oz soft silken tofu
45 ml/3 tbsp milk
10 ml/2 tsp mustard
2.5 ml/½ tsp white wine vinegar
cayenne pepper
salt and ground black pepper
radish roses and fresh herb sprigs,
   to garnish

1 Cut the avocado in half, remove the stone and strip off the skin. Cut the flesh into slices. Transfer to a plate, drizzle over the lime juice and set aside.

2 Wash and dry the baby spinach leaves. Put them in a mixing bowl.

3 Cut the larger cherry tomatoes in half and add all the tomatoes to the mixing bowl with the spring onions. Cut the cucumber into chunks and add to the bowl with the sliced radishes.

COOK'S TIP

Use soft silken tofu rather than the firm block variety. It can be found in most supermarkets in long-life cartons.

4 To make the dressing, put the tofu, milk, mustard, vinegar and a pinch of cayenne in a food processor or blender. Add salt and pepper to taste. Process for 30 seconds, until smooth. Scrape the dressing into a bowl and add a little extra milk if you like a thinner dressing. Sprinkle with a little extra cayenne, garnish with radish roses and herb sprigs and serve separately. Place the avocado slices with the spinach salad on a serving dish.

Radish, Mango and Apple Salad

Radish is a year-round vegetable and this salad, with its clean, crisp tastes and mellow flavours, can be served at any time of year. Serve with smoked fish, such as rolls of smoked salmon, or with continental ham or salami.

INGREDIENTS

Serves 4

10–15 radishes

1 apple, peeled, cored and thinly sliced

2 celery sticks, thinly sliced

1 small ripe mango

fresh dill sprigs, to garnish

For the dressing

120 ml/4 fl oz/½ cup soured cream

10 ml/2 tsp creamed horseradish

15 ml/1 tbsp chopped fresh dill

salt and ground black pepper

1 To prepare the dressing, blend together the soured cream, horseradish and dill in a small bowl and season with a little salt and pepper.

2 Top and tail the radishes and slice them thinly. Put in a bowl together with the apple and celery.

3 Halve the mango lengthways, cutting either side of the stone. Make even, criss-cross cuts through the flesh of each side section and bend it back to separate the cubes. Remove the cubes with a small knife and add to the bowl. Pour the dressing over the vegetables and fruit and stir gently so that all the ingredients are well coated. Garnish with dill sprigs and serve.

Mango, Tomato and Red Onion Salad

This salad makes an appetizing starter. The under-ripe mango blends well with the tomato.

INGREDIENTS

Serves 4

1 firm under-ripe mango

2 large tomatoes or 1 beef tomato, sliced

1/2 red onion, sliced into rings

1/2 cucumber, peeled and thinly sliced

For the dressing

30 ml/2 tbsp sunflower or vegetable oil

15 ml/1 tbsp lemon juice

1 garlic clove, crushed

2.5 ml/1/2 tsp hot pepper sauce

salt and ground black pepper

snipped chives, to garnish

1 Have the mango lengthways, cutting either side of the stone. Cut the flesh into slices and peel the skin away.

2 Arrange the mango, tomato, onion and cucumber on a large serving plate.

3 Blend the oil, lemon juice, garlic, pepper sauce and seasoning in a blender or food processor, or place in a small screw-top jar and shake vigorously.

4 Pour the dressing over the salad and serve garnished with snipped chives.

Orange and Water Chestnut Salad

Crunchy water chestnuts combine with radicchio or red lettuce and oranges in this unusual salad.

Serves 4

1 medium red onion, thinly sliced
    into rings
2 oranges, peeled and cut into segments
1 can drained water chestnuts, peeled and
    cut into strips
2 radicchio heads, cored, or 1 red-leaf
    lettuce, leaves separated
45 ml/3 tbsp chopped fresh parsley
45 ml/3 tbsp chopped fresh basil
15 ml/1 tbsp white wine vinegar
50 ml/2 fl oz/¼ cup walnut oil
salt and ground black pepper
1 fresh basil sprig, to garnish

1 Put the onion in a colander and sprinkle with 5 ml/1 tsp salt. Allow to drain for 15 minutes.

2 In a large mixing bowl combine the oranges and water chestnuts.

3 Spread out the radicchio or red-leaf lettuce leaves in a large, shallow bowl or on a serving platter.

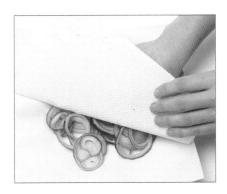

4 Rinse the onion to remove excess salt and dry on kitchen paper. Toss it with the water chestnuts and oranges.

5 Arrange the water chestnut, orange and onion mixture on top of the radicchio or lettuce leaves. Sprinkle with the chopped parsley and basil.

6 Put the vinegar, oil and salt and pepper to taste in a screw-top jar and shake well to combine. Pour the dressing over the salad and serve immediately, garnished with a sprig of basil.

Coleslaw with Pesto Mayonnaise

Both the pesto and the mayonnaise can be made for this dish. However, if time is short, you can buy them ready-prepared and it will taste just as good. Add the dressing just before serving to keep the cabbage crisp.

INGREDIENTS

Serves 4–6

1 small or ½ medium white cabbage

3–4 carrots, grated

4 spring onions, finely sliced

25–40 g/1–1½ oz/¼–⅓ cup pine nuts

15 ml/1 tbsp chopped fresh mixed herbs
    such as parsley, basil, chervil

For the pesto mayonnaise

1 egg yolk

about 10 ml/2 tsp lemon juice

200 ml/7 fl oz/scant 1 cup sunflower oil

10 ml/2 tsp pesto

60 ml/4 tbsp plain yogurt

salt and ground black pepper

1 To make the mayonnaise, place the egg yolk in a blender or food processor and process with the lemon juice. With the machine running, very slowly add the oil, pouring it more quickly as the mayonnaise emulsifies.

2 Season to taste with salt and pepper and a little more lemon juice if necessary. Alternatively, make the mayonnaise by hand using a balloon whisk.

3 Spoon 75 ml/5 tbsp of the mayonnaise into a bowl and stir in the pesto and yogurt, beating well to make a fairly thin dressing.

4 Remove the outer leaves of the cabbage and discard. Using a food processor or a sharp knife, thinly slice the cabbage and place in a large salad bowl.

5 Add the carrots and spring onions, together with the pine nuts and herbs, mixing thoroughly with your hands. Stir the pesto dressing into the salad or serve separately in a small dish.

Pepper and Cucumber Salad

Generous quantities of fresh herbs transform ordinary ingredients.

Serves 4

1 yellow or red pepper

1 large cucumber

4–5 tomatoes

1 bunch spring onions

30 ml/2 tbsp fresh parsley

30 ml/2 tbsp fresh mint

30 ml/2 tbsp fresh coriander

2 pitta breads, to serve

For the dressing

2 garlic cloves, crushed

75 ml/5 tbsp olive oil

juice of 2 lemons

salt and ground black pepper

1 Slice the pepper, discard the seeds and core. Roughly chop the cucumber and tomatoes. Place in a large salad bowl.

2 Trim and slice the spring onions. Add to the cucumber, tomatoes and pepper. Finely chop the parsley, mint and coriander and add to the bowl. If you have plenty of herbs, you can add as much as you like.

3 To make the dressing, blend the garlic with the olive oil and lemon juice in a jug, then season to taste with salt and pepper. Pour the dressing over the salad and toss lightly to mix.

4 Toast the pitta breads in a toaster or under a hot grill until crisp and serve them alongside the salad.

VARIATION

If you prefer, make this oriental salad in the traditional way. After toasting the pitta breads, crush them in your hand and then sprinkle over the salad before serving.

Guacamole Salsa in Red Leaves

This lovely, light, summery starter looks especially attractive arranged in individual cups of radicchio leaves. Serve with chunks of warm garlic bread.

INGREDIENTS

Serves 4

2 tomatoes

15 ml/1 tbsp grated onion

1 garlic clove, crushed

1 green chilli, halved, seeded and chopped

2 ripe avocados

30 ml/2 tbsp olive oil

2.5 ml/½ tsp ground cumin

30 ml/2 tbsp chopped fresh coriander
  or parsley

juice of 1 lime

radicchio leaves

salt and ground black pepper

fresh coriander sprigs, to garnish

crusty garlic bread and lime wedges,
  to serve

2 Put the tomato flesh into a bowl together with the onion, garlic and chilli. Halve the avocados, remove the stones, then scoop the flesh into the bowl, mashing it with a fork.

3 Add the oil, cumin, coriander or parsley and lime juice. Mix well together, seasoning to taste.

4 Lay the radicchio leaves on a platter and spoon in the salsa. Serve garnished with coriander sprigs and accompanied by garlic bread and lime wedges.

1 Using a sharp knife, slash a small cross on the top of the tomatoes, then place them in a bowl of boiling water for 30 seconds. The skins will slip off easily. Remove the core of each tomato and chop the flesh.

Thai Fruit and Vegetable Salad

A cooling, refreshing salad served with a coconut dipping sauce that has a slight kick.

Serves 4–6

1 small pineapple

1 small mango, peeled and sliced

1 green apple, cored and sliced

6 lychees, peeled and stoned

115 g/4 oz French beans, topped, tailed and halved

1 medium red onion, sliced

1 small cucumber, cut into short fingers

115 g/4 oz/½ cup beansprouts

2 spring onions, sliced

1 ripe tomato, quartered

225 g/8 oz cos or iceberg lettuce leaves

For the coconut dipping sauce

30 ml/2 tbsp coconut cream

30 ml/2 tbsp sugar

75 ml/5 tbsp/⅓ cup boiling water

1.5 ml/¼ tsp chilli sauce

15 ml/1 tbsp Thai fish sauce

juice of 1 lime

1 To make the coconut dipping sauce, put the coconut cream, sugar and boiling water in a screw-top jar. Add the chilli and fish sauces and lime juice and shake.

2 Trim both ends of the pineapple with a serrated knife, then cut away the outer skin.

Remove the central core with an apple corer. Alternatively, cut the pineapple into quarters down the middle and remove the core with a knife. Roughly chop the pineapple and set aside with the other fruits.

3 Bring a small saucepan of salted water to the boil and cook the beans for 3–4 minutes. Refresh under cold running water and set aside. To serve, arrange the fruits and vegetables in small heaps in a wide, shallow bowl. Serve the coconut sauce separately as a dip.

Sweet Cucumber Cooler

Sweet dipping sauces such as this bring instant relief to the hot chilli flavours of Thai food.

Makes 120ml/4fl oz/½ cup

5 tbsp water

2 tbsp sugar

½ tsp salt

1 tbsp rice or white wine vinegar

¼ small cucumber

2 shallots, or 1 small red onion

1 With a small sharp knife, thinly slice the cumber and cut into quarters. Thinly slice the shallots or red onion.

2 Measure the water, sugar, salt and vinegar into a stainless steel or enamel saucepan, bring to the boil and simmer until the sugar has dissolved, for less than 1 minute.

3 Allow to cool. Add the cumber and shallots or onion and serve at room temperature.

Tricolour Salad

This can be a simple starter if served on individual salad plates, or part of a light buffet meal laid out on a platter. When lightly salted, tomatoes make their own flavoursome dressing with their natural juices.

INGREDIENTS

Serves 4–6

1 small red onion, thinly sliced

6 large full-flavoured tomatoes

extra-virgin olive oil, to sprinkle

50 g/2 oz rocket or watercress leaves,
    roughly chopped

175 g/6 oz Mozzarella cheese, thinly sliced
    or grated

30 ml/2 tbsp pine nuts (optional)

salt and ground black pepper

1 Soak the onion slices in a bowl of cold water for 30 minutes, then drain and pat dry. Skin the tomatoes by cutting a cross in the skin and plunging into boiling water for 30 seconds: the skins can then be easily slipped off.

2 Slice the tomatoes and arrange half on a large platter, or divide them between small plates.

3 Sprinkle liberally with olive oil, then layer with the chopped rocket or watercress, onion slices and cheese, sprinkling over more oil and seasoning well between the layers.

4 Season well to finish and complete with some oil and a good scattering of pine nuts, if you wish. Cover the salad and chill for at least 2 hours before serving.

Tuscan Tuna and Bean Salad

A great store-cupboard dish which can be put together in very little time. Served with crusty bread, this salad makes a meal in itself.

INGREDIENTS

Serves 4

1 red onion

30 ml/2 tbsp smooth French mustard

300 ml/½ pint/1¼ cups olive oil

60 ml/4 tbsp white wine vinegar

30 ml/2 tbsp chopped fresh parsley

30 ml/2 tbsp chopped fresh chives

30 ml/2 tbsp chopped fresh tarragon
   or chervil

400 g/14 oz can haricot beans

400 g/14 oz can kidney beans

225 g/8 oz canned tuna in oil, drained and
   lightly flaked

fresh chives and tarragon sprigs,
   to garnish

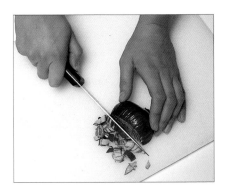

1 Chop the red onion finely, using a sharp knife.

2 To make the dressing, whisk together the mustard, oil, vinegar, parsley, chives and tarragon or chervil.

3 Drain the haricot and kidney beans through a colander, then rinse in fresh water.

4 Mix the chopped onion, beans and dressing together thoroughly, then carefully fold in the tuna. Garnish with chives and tarragon sprigs and serve.

Rocket, Pear and Parmesan Salad

For a sophisticated start to an elaborate meal, try this simple salad of honey-rich pears, fresh Parmesan and aromatic rocket leaves.

Serves 4

3 ripe pears (Williams or Packhams)
10 ml/2 tsp lemon juice
45 ml/3 tbsp hazelnut or walnut oil
115 g/4 oz rocket leaves
75 g/3 oz piece Parmesan cheese
ground black pepper

2 Combine the hazelnut or walnut oil with the pears. Add the rocket leaves and toss.

3 Turn the salad out on to four small plates and top with shavings of Parmesan cheese. Season with pepper and serve.

1 Peel and core the pears and slice thickly. Moisten with lemon juice to keep the flesh white.

COOK'S TIP

Parmesan cheese is a delicious main ingredient in a salad. Buy a chunk of fresh Parmesan and shave strips off the side, using a vegetable peeler. The distinctive flavour is quite strong. Store the rest of the Parmesan uncovered in the fridge.

Tomato and Feta Cheese Salad

Sweet, sun-ripened tomatoes are rarely more delicious than when served with feta cheese and olive oil.

INGREDIENTS

Serves 4

900 g/2 lb tomatoes

200 g/7 oz feta cheese

120 ml/4 fl oz/¹/₂ cup olive oil

12 black olives

4 fresh basil sprigs

ground black pepper

2 Slice the tomatoes thickly and arrange them attractively in a shallow serving dish.

3 Crumble the feta over the tomatoes, sprinkle with oil, then strew with the olives and basil sprigs. Season to taste with pepper and serve at room temperature.

1 Remove the tough cores from the tomatoes, using a small, sharp knife.

COOK'S TIP

Feta cheese has a strong flavour and can be salty. The least salty variety is imported from Greece and Turkey, and is available from specialist delicatessens.

COOKED SIDE
SALADS

Simple Cooked Salad

This version of a popular Mediterranean recipe is served as a side dish to accompany a main course.

Serves 4

2 well-flavoured tomatoes, quartered

2 onions, chopped

$\frac{1}{2}$ cucumber, halved lengthways, seeded and sliced

1 green pepper, halved, seeded and chopped

For the dressing

30 ml/2 tbsp lemon juice

45 ml/3 tbsp olive oil

2 garlic cloves, crushed

30 ml/2 tbsp chopped fresh coriander

salt and ground black pepper

1 Put the prepared tomatoes, onions, cucumber and green pepper into a large saucepan, add 60 ml/4 tbsp water and simmer for 5 minutes. Leave to cool.

2 For the dressing, mix together the lemon juice, olive oil and garlic. Strain the vegetables, then transfer to a serving bowl. Pour over the dressing, season with salt and pepper and stir in the chopped coriander. Serve at once, garnished with coriander sprigs.

Sweet-and-sour Artichoke Salad

A sweet-and-sour sauce, poured over lightly cooked summer vegetables, works perfectly in this delicious salad.

INGREDIENTS

Serves 4

6 small globe artichokes
juice of 1 lemon
30 ml/2 tbsp olive oil
2 medium onions, roughly chopped
175 g/6 oz/1½ cups fresh or frozen broad
   beans (shelled weight)
175 g/6 oz/1½ cups fresh or frozen peas
   (shelled weight)
salt and ground black pepper
fresh mint leaves, to garnish

For the sweet-and-sour sauce
120 ml/4 fl oz/½ cup white wine vinegar
15 ml/1 tbsp caster sugar
a handful of fresh mint leaves,
   roughly torn

1 Peel the outer leaves from the artichokes and discard. Cut the artichokes into quarters and place them in a bowl of water with the lemon juice.

2 Heat the olive oil in a large saucepan and add the onions. Cook until the onions are golden. Add the beans and stir, then drain the artichokes and add to the pan. Pour in about 300 ml/½ pint/ 1¼ cups water and cook, covered, for a further 10–15 minutes.

3 Add the peas, season with salt and pepper and cook for a further 5 minutes, stirring from time to time, until the vegetables are tender. Strain through a sieve or colander and place all the vegetables in a bowl. Leave to cool, then cover and chill.

4 To make the sweet-and-sour sauce, mix all the ingredients in a small pan. Heat gently for 2–3 minutes, until the sugar has dissolved. Simmer gently for about 5 minutes, stirring occasionally. Leave to cool. To serve, drizzle the sauce over the vegetables and garnish with mint leaves.

Tomato, Savory and French Bean Salad

Savory and beans could have been invented for each other. This salad mixes them with ripe tomatoes, making a superb accompaniment for cold meats.

INGREDIENTS

Serves 4

450 g/1 lb French beans

1 kg/2¼ lb ripe tomatoes

3 spring onions, roughly sliced

15 ml/1 tbsp pine nuts

4 fresh savory sprigs

For the dressing

30 ml/2 tbsp extra-virgin olive oil

juice of 1 lime

75 g/3 oz Dolcelatte cheese

1 garlic clove, peeled and crushed

salt and ground black pepper

1 Prepare the dressing first so that it can stand for a while before use. Place all the dressing ingredients in the bowl of a food processor, season to taste and blend until the cheese is finely chopped and you have a smooth dressing. Pour it into a jug.

2 Top and tail the beans, and boil in salted water until they are just cooked.

3 Drain the beans and run cold water over them until they have completely cooled. Slice the tomatoes, or, if they are fairly small, quarter them.

4 Toss the beans, tomatoes and spring onions. Pour on the dressing, sprinkle the pine nuts and savory sprigs over the top and serve.

Squash à la Grecque

This recipe, usually made with mushrooms, also works well with patty-pan squash. Make sure that you cook the baby squash until they are quite tender, so they absorb the delicious flavours of the marinade.

Serves 4

175 g/6 oz patty-pan squash

250 ml/8 fl oz/1 cup white wine

juice of 2 lemons

1 fresh thyme sprig

1 bay leaf, plus extra to garnish

small bunch of fresh chervil,
   roughly chopped

1.5 ml/¼ tsp crushed coriander seeds

1.5 ml/¼ tsp crushed black peppercorns

75 ml/5 tbsp olive oil

extra bay leaves, to garnish

1 Blanch the patty-pan squash in boiling water for 3 minutes, then refresh them in cold water.

2 Place all the remaining ingredients in a pan, add 150 ml/¼ pint/⅔ cup water and simmer for 10 minutes, covered. Add the squash and cook for 10 minutes until they are tender. Remove with a slotted spoon.

3 Reduce the liquid by boiling hard for 10 minutes. Strain and pour it over the squash. Leave until cool for the flavours to be absorbed. Serve cold, garnished with bay leaves.

Warm Broad Bean and Feta Salad

This medley of fresh-tasting salad ingredients is lovely warm or cold as a starter or accompaniment to a main course.

INGREDIENTS

Serves 4–6

900 g/2 lb broad beans, shelled, or
    350 g/12 oz shelled frozen beans

60 ml/4 tbsp olive oil

175 g/6 oz fresh plum tomatoes, halved,
    or quartered if large

4 garlic cloves, crushed

115 g/4 oz firm feta cheese, cut
    into chunks

45 ml/3 tbsp chopped fresh dill

12 black olives

salt and ground black pepper

chopped fresh dill, to garnish

1 Cook the broad beans in boiling, salted water until just tender. Drain and set aside.

2 Meanwhile, heat the olive oil in a heavy-based frying pan and add the tomatoes and garlic. Cook until the tomatoes are beginning to change colour.

3 Add the feta to the pan and toss the ingredients together for 1 minute. Mix with the drained beans, dill, olives and salt and pepper. Serve garnished with chopped dill.

COOK'S TIP

Plum tomatoes are now widely available in supermarkets fresh as well as tinned. Their deep red, oval shapes are very attractive in salads and they have a sweet, rich flavour.

Halloumi and Grape Salad

In this recipe firm, salty halloumi cheese is fried and then tossed with sweet, juicy grapes which really complement its distinctive flavour.

INGREDIENTS

Serves 4

150 g/5 oz mixed green salad leaves

75 g/3 oz seedless green grapes

75 g/3 oz seedless black grapes

250 g/9 oz halloumi cheese

45 ml/3 tbsp olive oil

fresh young thyme leaves or fresh dill,
    to garnish

For the dressing

60 ml/4 tbsp olive oil

15 ml/1 tbsp lemon juice

2.5 ml/½ tsp caster sugar

15 ml/1 tbsp chopped fresh thyme or dill

salt and ground black pepper

1 To make the dressing, mix together the olive oil, lemon juice and sugar. Season with salt and pepper. Stir in the chopped thyme or dill and set aside.

2 Toss together the salad leaves and the green and black grapes, then transfer to a large serving plate.

3 Thinly slice the cheese. Heat the oil in a large frying pan. Add the cheese and fry briefly until golden on the underside. Turn the cheese with a fish slice and cook the other side.

4 Arrange the cheese over the salad. Pour over the dressing and garnish with sprigs of fresh thyme or dill.

Poached Egg Salad with Croûtons

Soft poached eggs, hot garlic croûtons and cool, crisp salad leaves make a great combination.

INGREDIENTS

Serves 2

½ small loaf white bread

75 ml/5 tbsp/⅓ cup extra-virgin olive oil

2 eggs

115 g/4 oz mixed salad leaves

2 garlic cloves, crushed

7.5 ml/½ tbsp white wine vinegar

25 g/1 oz piece Parmesan cheese

ground black pepper

1 Remove the crust from the loaf of bread. Cut the bread into 2.5 cm/1 in cubes.

2 Heat 30 ml/2 tbsp of the oil in a frying pan. Cook the bread for about 5 minutes, tossing the cubes occasionally, until they are golden brown.

3 Meanwhile, bring a pan of water to the boil. Carefully slide in the eggs, one at a time. Gently poach the eggs for 4 minutes until lightly cooked.

4 Divide the salad leaves between two plates. Remove the croûtons from the frying pan and arrange them over the leaves. Wipe the frying pan clean with kitchen paper.

5 Heat the remaining oil in the pan, add the garlic and vinegar and cook over a high heat for 1 minute. Pour the warm dressing over each salad.

6 Place a poached egg on each plate of salad. Scatter with shavings of Parmesan and a little black pepper.

COOK'S TIP

Add a dash of vinegar to the water before poaching the eggs. This helps to keep the whites together.

To ensure that a poached egg has a good shape, swirl the water with a spoon, whirlpool-fashion, before sliding in the egg.

Before serving trim the edges of the egg for a neat finish.

Roasted Pepper and Tomato Salad

A lovely, colourful recipe which perfectly combines several red ingredients. Eat this dish at room temperature with a green salad.

INGREDIENTS

Serves 4

3 red peppers

6 large plum tomatoes

2.5 ml/½ tsp dried red chilli flakes

1 red onion, finely sliced

3 garlic cloves, finely chopped

grated rind and juice of 1 lemon

45 ml/3 tbsp chopped fresh
    flat-leaf parsley

30 ml/2 tbsp extra-virgin olive oil

salt and ground black pepper

black and green olives and extra chopped
    flat-leaf parsley, to garnish

1 Preheat the oven to 220°C/425°F/Gas 7. Place the peppers on a baking sheet and roast, turning occasionally, for 10 minutes or until the skins are almost blackened. Add the tomatoes to the baking sheet and bake for 5 minutes more.

2 Place the peppers in a strong polythene bag, close the top loosely, trapping in the steam. Set aside, with the tomatoes, until cool enough to handle.

3 Carefully pull the skin off the peppers. Remove the core and seeds, then chop the peppers and tomatoes roughly and place in a mixing bowl.

4 Add the chilli flakes, onion, garlic, lemon rind and juice. Sprinkle over the parsley. Mix well, then transfer to a serving dish. Sprinkle with a little salt and black pepper, drizzle over the olive oil and scatter the olives and extra parsley over the top. Serve at room temperature.

Marinated Courgettes

This is a simple vegetable dish which uses the best of the season's courgettes. It can be eaten either hot or cold.

INGREDIENTS

Serves 4

4 courgettes

60 ml/4 tbsp extra-virgin olive oil

30 ml/2 tbsp chopped fresh mint

30 ml/2 tbsp white wine vinegar

salt and ground black pepper

fresh mint leaves, to garnish

wholemeal Italian bread and green olives,
    to serve

1 Cut the courgettes into thin slices. Heat 30 ml/2 tbsp of the oil in a wide, heavy-based saucepan. Fry the courgettes in batches, for 4–6 minutes, until tender and brown around the edges. Transfer the courgettes to a bowl. Season well.

2 Heat the remaining oil in the pan, then add the chopped mint and vinegar and let it bubble for a few seconds. Pour over the courgettes. Marinate for 1 hour, then serve garnished with mint leaves and accompanied by bread and olives.

Green Bean and Sweet Red Pepper Salad

A galaxy of colour and texture, with a jolt of heat from the chilli, will make this a favourite salad.

Serves 4

350 g/12 oz cooked green beans, quartered

2 red peppers, seeded and chopped

2 spring onions (both white and green parts), chopped

1 or more drained pickled serrano chillies, well rinsed, seeded and chopped

1 iceberg lettuce, coarsely shredded, or mixed salad leaves

green olives, to garnish

For the dressing

45 ml/3 tbsp red wine vinegar

135 ml/9 tbsp olive oil

salt and ground black pepper

1 Combine the green beans, peppers, spring onions and chilli(es) in a salad bowl.

2 To make the dressing, pour the vinegar into a bowl or jug. Add salt and pepper to taste, then gradually whisk in the olive oil until well combined.

3 Pour the dressing over the prepared vegetables and toss lightly together to mix and coat thoroughly.

4 Line a large serving platter with the shredded lettuce or mixed salad leaves and arrange the vegetable mixture attractively on top. Garnish with the olives and serve.

Green Green Salad

You could make this lovely dish any time of the year with frozen vege-tables and still get a pretty salad.

INGREDIENTS

Serves 4

175 g/6 oz shelled broad beans

115 g/4 oz French beans, quartered

115 g/4 oz mangetouts

8–10 small fresh mint leaves

3 spring onions, chopped

For the dressing

60 ml/4 tbsp green olive oil

15 ml/1 tbsp cider vinegar

15 ml/1 tbsp chopped fresh mint

1 garlic clove, crushed

salt and ground black pepper

1 Plunge the broad beans into a saucepan of boiling water and bring back to the boil. Remove from the heat immediately and plunge into cold water. Drain. Repeat with the French beans.

COOK'S TIP

Frozen broad beans are a good stand-by, but for this salad it is worth shelling fresh beans for the extra flavour.

2 In a large bowl, mix the blanched broad beans and French beans with the raw mangetouts, mint leaves and spring onions.

3 In another bowl, mix together the olive oil, vinegar, chopped or dried mint, garlic and seasoning. Pour over the salad and toss well. Chill until ready to serve.

Leek and Egg Salad

Smooth-textured leeks are especially delicious warm when partnered with an earthy-rich sauce of parsley, olive oil and walnuts. Serve as a side salad with plainly-grilled or poached fish and new potatoes.

INGREDIENTS

Serves 4

675 g/1½ lb young leeks

1 egg

fresh parsley sprigs, to garnish

For the dressing

25 g/1 oz fresh parsley

30 ml/2 tbsp olive oil

juice of ½ lemon

50 g/2 oz/½ cup broken walnuts, toasted

5 ml/1 tsp caster sugar

salt and ground black pepper

2 Lower the egg into boiling water and cook for 12 minutes. Cool under running water, shell and set aside.

3 To make the dressing, finely chop the parsley in a food processor.

4 Add the olive oil, lemon juice and toasted walnuts. Blend for 1–2 minutes, until smooth.

5 Adjust the consistency with about 90 ml/6 tbsp water. Add the sugar and season to taste with salt and pepper.

6 Place the leeks on an attractive plate, then spoon on the sauce. Finely grate the hard-boiled egg and scatter over the sauce. Garnish with the reserved parsley sprigs and serve while the leeks are still warm.

1 Bring a saucepan of salted water to the boil. Cut the leeks into 10 cm/4 in lengths and rinse well to flush out any grit or soil. Cook the leeks for 8 minutes. Drain and part-cool under running water.

Winter Vegetable Salad

This simple side salad is made with leeks, cauliflower and celery, flavoured with white wine, herbs and juniper berries.

Serves 4

175 ml/6 fl oz/¾ cup white wine
5 ml/1 tsp olive oil
30 ml/2 tbsp lemon juice
2 bay leaves
1 fresh thyme sprig
4 juniper berries
450 g/1 lb leeks, trimmed and cut into
   2.5 cm/1 in lengths
1 small cauliflower, broken into florets
4 celery sticks, sliced on the diagonal
30 ml/2 tbsp chopped fresh parsley
salt and ground black pepper

1 Put the wine, olive oil, lemon juice, bay leaves, thyme and juniper berries into a large, heavy-based saucepan and bring to the boil. Cover and leave to simmer for 20 minutes.

2 Add the leeks, cauliflower and celery. Simmer very gently for 5–6 minutes, or until just tender.

3 Remove the vegetables with a slotted spoon and transfer them to a serving dish. Briskly boil the cooking liquid for 15–20 minutes, or until reduced by half. Strain through a sieve.

4 Stir the parsley into the liquid and season to taste. Pour over the vegetables and leave to cool. Chill in the fridge for at least 1 hour before serving.

COOK'S TIP

Vary the vegetables
for this salad according to
the season.

Avocado and Smoked Fish Salad

Avocado and smoked fish make a good combination and, flavoured with herbs and spices, create a delectable salad.

INGREDIENTS

Serves 4

2 avocados

½ cucumber

15 ml/1 tbsp lemon juice

2 firm tomatoes

1 green chilli

salt and ground black pepper

For the fish

15 g/½ oz/1 tbsp butter or margarine

½ onion, finely sliced

5 ml/1 tsp mustard seeds

225 g/8 oz smoked mackerel, flaked

30 ml/2 tbsp fresh chopped
    coriander leaves

2 firm tomatoes, peeled and chopped

15 ml/1 tbsp lemon juice

1 For the fish, melt the butter or margarine in a frying pan, add the onion and mustard seeds and fry for about 5 minutes, until the onion is soft.

2 Add the mackerel, coriander, tomatoes and lemon juice and cook over a low heat for 2–3 minutes. Remove from the heat and leave to cool.

3 To make the salad, slice the avocados and cucumber thinly. Place together in a bowl and sprinkle with the lemon juice. Slice the tomatoes and seed them. Finely chop the chilli.

4 Place the fish mixture in the centre of a serving plate.

5 Arrange the avocados, cucumber and tomatoes decoratively around the outside. Alternatively, spoon a quarter of the fish mixture on to each of four serving plates and divide the avocados, cucumber and tomatoes equally between them. Sprinkle with the chopped chilli and a little salt and pepper and serve.

VARIATION

Smoked haddock or cod can also be used in this salad, or a mixture of mackerel and haddock.

Tomato and Bread Salad

This salad, which conveniently uses up stale bread, is best made with flavourful, sun-ripened tomatoes.

INGREDIENTS

Serves 4

400 g/14 oz stale white or brown bread
   or rolls
4 large tomatoes
1 large red onion or 6 spring onions
a few fresh basil leaves, to garnish

For the dressing

60 ml/4 tbsp extra-virgin olive oil
30 ml/2 tbsp white wine vinegar
salt and ground black pepper

1 Cut the bread or rolls into thick slices. Place in a shallow bowl and soak with cold water. Leave for at least 30 minutes.

2 Cut the tomatoes into chunks and place in a serving bowl. Finely slice the onion or spring onions and add them to the tomatoes. Squeeze as much water out of the bread as possible and add it to the vegetables.

3 To make the dressing, mix the oil and vinegar. Season with salt and pepper, pour over the salad and mix well. Garnish with the basil leaves. Allow to stand in a cool place for at least 2 hours before serving.

Grilled Pepper Salad

Ideally this salad should be made with a combination of red and yellow peppers for the most jewel-like, colourful effect and the sweetest flavour.

INGREDIENTS

Serves 6

4 large peppers, red or yellow or a
   combination of both
30 ml/2 tbsp capers, rinsed
18–20 black or green olives

For the dressing

90 ml/6 tbsp extra-virgin olive oil
2 garlic cloves, finely chopped
30 ml/2 tbsp balsamic or wine vinegar
salt and ground black pepper

1 Place the peppers under a hot grill and turn occasionally until they are black and blistered on all sides. Remove from the heat, place in a strong polythene bag and close the top loosely. Set aside until they are cool enough to handle. Carefully peel the peppers, then cut them into quarters. Remove the stems and seeds.

2 Cut the peppers into strips, and arrange them on a serving dish. Distribute the capers and olives evenly over the peppers.

3 For the dressing, mix the oil and garlic in a small bowl, crushing the garlic with a spoon to release the flavour. Mix in the vinegar and season with salt and pepper. Pour over the salad, mix well and allow to stand for at least 30 minutes before serving.

Curly Endive Salad with Bacon

This delicious salad may also be sprinkled with chopped hard-boiled egg.

INGREDIENTS

Serves 4

50 g/2 oz white bread

225 g/8 oz curly endive or escarole leaves

75–90 ml/5–6 tbsp extra-virgin olive oil

175 g/6 oz piece smoked bacon, diced, or 6 thick-cut smoked bacon rashers, cut crossways into thin strips

1 small garlic clove, finely chopped

15 ml/1 tbsp red wine vinegar

10 ml/2 tsp Dijon mustard

salt and ground black pepper

1 Cut the bread into small cubes. Tear the endive or escarole into bite-size pieces and put into a salad bowl.

2 Heat 15 ml/1 tbsp of the oil in a medium, non-stick frying pan over a medium-low heat and add the bacon. Fry gently until well browned, stirring occasionally. Remove the bacon with a slotted spoon and drain on kitchen paper.

3 Add another 30 ml/2 tbsp of the oil to the pan and fry the bread cubes over a medium-high heat, turning frequently, until evenly browned. Remove the bread cubes with a slotted spoon and drain on kitchen paper. Discard any remaining fat.

4 Stir the garlic, vinegar and mustard into the pan with the remaining oil and heat until just warm, whisking to combine. Season to taste, then pour the dressing over the salad and sprinkle with the fried bacon and croûtons. Serve immediately while still warm.

Asparagus and Orange Salad

A slightly unusual combination of ingredients with a simple dressing based on good-quality olive oil.

Serves 4

225 g/8 oz asparagus, trimmed and cut
    into 5 cm/2 in lengths

2 large oranges

2 well-flavoured tomatoes, cut
    into eighths

50 g/2 oz cos lettuce leaves

30 ml/2 tbsp extra-virgin olive oil

2.5 ml/½ tsp sherry vinegar

salt and ground black pepper

1 Cook the asparagus in boiling, salted water for 3–4 minutes, until just tender. The cooking time may vary according to the size of the asparagus stems. Drain and refresh under cold water, then leave on one side to cool.

2 Grate the rind from half an orange and reserve. Peel both the oranges and cut into segments. Squeeze the juice from the membrane and reserve.

3 Put the asparagus, orange segments, tomatoes and lettuce into a salad bowl.

5 ml/1 tsp of the grated rind. Season with salt and pepper. Just before serving, pour the dressing over the salad and mix gently to coat all the ingredients.

4 Mix together the oil and vinegar, and add 15 ml/1 tbsp of the reserved orange juice and

Hard-boiled Eggs with Tuna Sauce

A tasty tuna mayonnaise poured over hard-boiled eggs makes a nourishing first course that is quick and easy to prepare.

INGREDIENTS

Serves 6

6 extra-large eggs

200 g/7 oz can tuna in olive oil

3 canned anchovy fillets

15 ml/1 tbsp capers, drained

30 ml/2 tbsp lemon juice

60 ml/4 tbsp olive oil

salt and ground black pepper

capers and anchovy fillets, to garnish

For the mayonnaise

1 egg yolk

5 ml/1 tsp Dijon mustard

5 ml/1 tsp white wine vinegar or
   lemon juice

150 ml/¼ pint/⅔ cup olive oil

1 Boil the eggs for 12–14 minutes. Drain them under cold water. Shell the eggs carefully and set aside.

2 Make the mayonnaise by whisking the egg yolk, mustard and vinegar or lemon juice together in a small bowl.

3 Whisk in the oil a few drops at a time until 3–4 tablespoons have been incorporated. Pour in the remaining oil in a slow stream, whisking constantly.

4 Place the tuna with its oil, the anchovies, capers, lemon juice and olive oil in a blender or food processor. Process until the mixture is smooth.

5 Fold the tuna mixture carefully into the mayonnaise. Season with black pepper, and salt if necessary. Chill for at least 1 hour.

6 Cut the eggs in half lengthways. Arrange on a serving platter. Spoon on the mayonnaise and garnish with capers and anchovy fillets. Serve chilled.

Artichoke and Egg Salad

Artichoke hearts are best when cut from fresh artichokes, but can also be bought frozen. This salad is easily assembled for a light lunch.

INGREDIENTS

Serves 4

4 large artichokes or 4 frozen artichoke
   hearts, thawed
½ lemon
4 eggs, hard-boiled and shelled
fresh parsley sprigs, to garnish

For the mayonnaise
1 egg yolk
10 ml/2 tsp Dijon mustard
15 ml/1 tbsp white wine vinegar
250 ml/8 fl oz/1 cup olive or vegetable oil
30 ml/2 tbsp chopped fresh parsley
salt and ground black pepper

1 If using fresh artichokes, wash them. Squeeze the lemon and put the juice and the squeezed half in a bowl of cold water.

2 Prepare the artichokes one at a time. Cut off only the tip from the stem. Peel the stem with a small knife, pulling upwards towards the leaves. Pull off the small leaves around the stem and continue snapping off the upper part of the dark outer leaves until you reach the taller inner leaves. Cut the tops off the leaves with a sharp knife. Place the artichoke in the acidulated water. Repeat with the other artichokes.

3 Boil or steam fresh artichokes until just tender (when a leaf comes away quite easily when pulled). Cook frozen artichoke hearts according to the packet instructions. Allow to cool.

4 To make the mayonnaise, combine the egg yolk, mustard and vinegar in a mixing bowl. Add salt and pepper to taste. Add the oil in a thin stream while beating vigorously with a wire whisk. When the mixture is thick and smooth, stir in the chopped parsley. Blend well. Cover and refrigerate until needed.

5 If using fresh artichokes, pull off the leaves. Cut the stems off level with the base. Scrape off the hairy "choke" with a knife or spoon.

6 Cut the eggs and artichokes into wedges. Arrange on a serving plate, spoon the mayonnaise over the top, garnish with parsley sprigs and serve.

Panzanella

In this lively salad, a sweet, tangy blend of tomato juice, rich olive oil and red wine vinegar is soaked up by a colourful mixture of roasted peppers, anchovies and toasted ciabatta bread.

INGREDIENTS

Serves 4–6

225 g/8 oz ciabatta (about ⅔ loaf)

150 ml/¼ pint/⅔ cup olive oil

3 red peppers

3 yellow peppers

50 g/2 oz can anchovy fillets, drained

675 g/1½ lb ripe plum tomatoes

4 garlic cloves, crushed

60 ml/4 tbsp red wine vinegar

50 g/2 oz capers

115 g/4 oz/1 cup pitted black olives

salt and ground black pepper

fresh basil leaves, to garnish

1 Preheat the oven to 200°C/400°F/Gas 6. Cut the ciabatta into 2 cm/¾ in chunks and drizzle with 50 ml/2 fl oz/¼ cup of the oil. Grill lightly until just golden.

2 Put the peppers on a foil-lined baking sheet and bake for about 45 minutes, until the skins begin to char. Remove the peppers from the oven, place in a strong plastic bag, close the end and leave to cool slightly.

3 Pull the skins off the peppers and cut them into quarters, discarding the stalk ends and seeds. Roughly chop the anchovies and set aside.

4 To make the tomato dressing, peel and halve the tomatoes. Scoop the seeds and pulp into a sieve set over a bowl. Using the back of a spoon, press the tomato pulp in the sieve to extract as much juice as possible. Discard the pulp and add the remaining oil, the garlic and vinegar to the juices.

5 Layer the toasted ciabatta, peppers, tomatoes, anchovies, capers and olives in a large salad bowl. Season the tomato dressing with salt and pepper and pour it over the salad. Leave to stand for about 30 minutes. Serve garnished with plenty of basil leaves.

Radicchio, Artichoke and Walnut Salad

The distinctive, earthy taste of Jerusalem artichokes makes a lovely contrast to the sharp freshness of radicchio and lemon. Serve warm or cold as an accompaniment to grilled steak or barbecued meats.

INGREDIENTS

Serves 4

1 large radicchio or 150 g/5 oz radicchio leaves

40 g/1½ oz/⅓ cup walnut pieces

45 ml/3 tbsp walnut oil

500 g/1¼ lb Jerusalem artichokes

thinly pared rind and juice of 1 lemon

coarse sea salt and ground black pepper

fresh flat-leaf parsley, to garnish

1 If using a whole radicchio, cut it into 8–10 wedges. Put the wedges or leaves in a flameproof dish. Scatter over the walnuts, then spoon over the oil and season. Grill for 2–3 minutes.

2 Peel the artichokes and cut up any large ones so that the pieces are all roughly the same size. Add the artichokes to a pan of boiling salted water with half the lemon juice and cook for 5–7 minutes, until tender. Drain. Preheat the grill to high.

3 Toss the artichokes into the salad with the remaining lemon juice and the pared rind. Season with coarse salt and pepper. Grill until beginning to brown. Serve at once garnished with torn pieces of parsley, if you like.

Egg, Bacon and Avocado Salad

A glorious medley of colours, flavours and textures to delight the eye and the taste buds.

INGREDIENTS

Serves 4

1 large cos lettuce

8 bacon rashers, fried until crisp

2 large avocados, peeled and diced

6 hard-boiled eggs, chopped

2 beef tomatoes, peeled, seeded
  and chopped

175 g/6 oz blue cheese, crumbled

For the dressing

1 garlic clove, crushed

5 ml/1 tsp sugar

7.5 ml/1½ tsp lemon juice

25 ml/1½ tbsp red wine vinegar

120 ml/4 fl oz/½ cup groundnut oil

salt and ground black pepper

1 Slice the lettuce into strips across the leaves. Crumble the fried bacon rashers.

2 To make the dressing, combine all the ingredients in a screw-top jar and shake well. On a large, rectangular or oval platter, spread out the strips of lettuce to make a bed.

3 Arrange the avocados, eggs, tomatoes and cheese neatly in rows on top of the lettuce. Sprinkle the bacon on top.

4 Pour the dressing carefully and evenly over the salad just before serving.

Spicy Sweetcorn Salad

This brilliant, sweet-flavoured salad is served warm with a delicious, spicy dressing.

INGREDIENTS

Serves 4

30 ml/2 tbsp vegetable oil

450 g/1 lb drained canned sweetcorn, or
  frozen sweetcorn, thawed

1 green pepper, seeded and diced

1 small red chilli, seeded and finely diced

4 spring onions, sliced

45 ml/3 tbsp chopped fresh parsley

225 g/8 oz cherry tomatoes, halved

salt and ground black pepper

For the dressing

2.5 ml/½ tsp sugar

30 ml/2 tbsp white wine vinegar

2.5 ml/½ tsp Dijon mustard

15 ml/1 tbsp chopped fresh basil

15 ml/1 tbsp mayonnaise

1.5 ml/¼ tsp chilli sauce

1 Heat the oil in a frying pan. Add the sweetcorn, green pepper, chilli and spring onions. Cook over a medium heat for about 5 minutes, until softened, stirring frequently.

2 Transfer the vegetables to a salad bowl. Stir in the parsley and the cherry tomatoes.

3 To make the dressing, combine all the ingredients in a small bowl and whisk together.

4 Pour the dressing over the sweetcorn mixture. Season with salt and pepper. Toss well to combine, then serve immediately, while the salad is still warm.

Tofu and Cucumber Salad

A nutritious and refreshing salad with a hot, sweet-and-sour dressing, this is ideal for buffets.

INGREDIENTS

Serves 4–6

1 small cucumber

115 g/4 oz square tofu

oil, for frying

115 g/4 oz/½ cup beansprouts

salt

celery leaves, to garnish

For the dressing

1 small onion, grated

2 garlic cloves, crushed

5–7.5 ml/1–1½ tsp chilli sauce

30–45 ml/2–3 tbsp dark soy sauce

15–30 ml/1–2 tbsp rice-wine vinegar

10 ml/2 tsp dark brown sugar

1 Cut the cucumber into neat cubes. Sprinkle with salt to extract excess liquid. Set aside, while preparing the remaining ingredients.

2 Cut the tofu into cubes. Heat a little oil in a pan and fry on both sides until golden brown. Drain on kitchen paper.

3 To make the dressing, blend together the onion, garlic and chilli sauce in a screw-top jar. Stir in the soy sauce, vinegar, sugar and salt to taste.

4 Just before serving, rinse the cucumber under cold running water. Drain and dry thoroughly. Toss the cucumber, tofu and beansprouts together in a serving bowl and pour over the dressing. Garnish with the celery leaves and serve the salad at once.

Plantain and Green Banana Salad

Cook the plantains and bananas in their skins to retain their soft texture. They will then absorb all the flavour of the dressing.

INGREDIENTS

Serves 4

2 firm yellow plantains

3 green bananas

1 garlic clove, crushed

1 red onion

15–30 ml/1–2 tbsp chopped fresh
  coriander

45 ml/3 tbsp sunflower oil

25 ml/1½ tbsp malt vinegar

salt and ground black pepper

1 Slit the plantains and bananas lengthways along their natural ridges, then cut in half and place in a large saucepan.

2 Cover the plantains and bananas with water, add a little salt and bring to the boil. Boil gently for 20 minutes, until tender, then remove from the water. When they are cool enough to handle, peel and cut into medium-size slices.

3 Put the plantain and banana slices into a bowl and add the garlic, turning them with a wooden spoon to distribute the garlic evenly.

4 Halve the onion and slice thinly. Add to the bowl with the coriander, oil, vinegar and seasoning. Toss together to mix, then transfer to a serving bowl.

Sweet Potato and Carrot Salad

This warm salad has a sweet-and-sour taste, and several unusual ingredients. It is attractively garnished with whole walnuts, sultanas and onion rings.

INGREDIENTS

Serves 4

1 medium sweet potato

2 carrots, cut into thick diagonal slices

3 medium tomatoes

8–10 iceberg lettuce leaves

75 g/3 oz/¹⁄₂ cup canned chick-peas, drained

For the dressing

15 ml/1 tbsp clear honey

90 ml/6 tbsp plain yogurt

2.5 ml/¹⁄₂ tsp salt

5 ml/1 tsp ground black pepper

For the garnish

15 ml/1 tbsp walnuts

15 ml/1 tbsp sultanas

1 small onion, cut into rings

1 Peel the sweet potato and cut roughly into cubes. Boil it until it is soft but not mushy, then cover the pan and set aside.

2 Boil the carrots for just a few minutes, making sure that they remain crunchy. Add the carrots to the sweet potato.

3 Drain the water from the sweet potato and carrots and place them together in a bowl.

4 Slice the tops off the tomatoes, then scoop out the seeds with a spoon and discard. Roughly chop the flesh. Slice the lettuce into strips across the leaves.

5 Line a salad bowl with the shredded lettuce leaves. Mix together the sweet potato, carrots, chick-peas and tomatoes and place the mixture in the centre.

6 To make the dressing, mix together all the ingredients and beat well, using a fork.

7 Garnish the salad with the walnuts, sultanas and onion rings. Pour the dressing over the top just before serving, or serve it in a separate bowl.

COOK'S TIP

This salad makes an excellent main course for lunch or a family supper. Serve it with a sweet mango chutney and warm naan bread.

Potato Salads

Most people adore home-made potato salad made with a creamy mayonnaise. These two versions are lighter and more summery. The first salad should be served warm; the second can be prepared a day ahead and served cold.

INGREDIENTS

Serves 4

900 g/2 lb new potatoes

5 ml/1 tsp salt

For the dressing for the warm salad

30 ml/2 tbsp hazelnut or walnut oil

60 ml/4 tbsp sunflower oil

juice of 1 lemon

15 pistachio nuts

salt and ground black pepper

flat-leaf parsley, to garnish

For the dressing for the cold salad

75 ml/5 tbsp olive oil

10 ml/2 tsp white wine vinegar

1 garlic clove, crushed

90 ml/6 tbsp finely chopped fresh parsley

2 large spring onions, finely chopped

salt and ground black pepper

1 Scrub the potatoes but don't peel them. Cover with cold water and bring to the boil. Add the salt and simmer for about 15 minutes, until tender. Drain the potatoes well and set aside.

2 For the warm salad, mix together the hazelnut or walnut oil with the sunflower oil and lemon juice and season well.

3 Use a knife to crush the pistachio nuts roughly.

4 When the potatoes have cooled slightly, pour over the dressing and sprinkle with the chopped nuts. Serve garnished with a sprig of parsley.

5 For the cold salad, cook the potatoes as above, drain and leave to cool.

6 Whisk together the oil, vinegar, garlic, parsley, spring onions and seasoning and pour over the potatoes. Cover tightly and chill overnight. Allow to come to room temperature before serving.

Potato Salad with Egg and Lemon Dressing

Potato salads are a popular addition to any salad spread and are enjoyed with an assortment of cold meats and fish. This recipe draws on the contrasting flavours of egg and lemon. Chopped parsley provides a fresh green finish.

INGREDIENTS

Serves 4

900 g/2 lb new potatoes

1 medium onion, finely chopped

1 hard-boiled egg

300 ml/½ pint/1¼ cups mayonnaise

1 garlic clove, crushed

finely grated rind and juice of 1 lemon

60 ml/4 tbsp chopped fresh parsley

salt and ground black pepper

fresh parsley sprig, to garnish

1 Scrub or scrape the potatoes, cover with cold water and bring to the boil. Add salt and simmer for 15 minutes, until tender. Drain and allow to cool. Cut the potatoes into large dice, season well and combine with the chopped onion.

2 Shell the hard-boiled egg and grate into a mixing bowl, then add the mayonnaise. Combine the garlic and lemon rind and juice in a small bowl and stir them carefully into the mayonnaise.

3 Mix the mayonnaise mixture thoroughly into the potatoes, then fold in the chopped parsley. Serve warm or cold, garnished with a sprig of parsley.

VARIATION

Fresh chives make an excellent alternative to parsley.

Spicy Potato Salad

This tasty salad is quick to prepare, and makes a satisfying accompaniment to grilled or barbecued meat or fish.

INGREDIENTS

Serves 6

900 g/2 lb potatoes

2 red peppers

2 celery sticks

1 shallot

2 or 3 spring onions

1 green chilli

1 garlic clove, crushed

10 ml/2 tsp finely snipped fresh chives

10 ml/2 tsp finely chopped fresh basil

15 ml/1 tbsp finely chopped fresh parsley

15 ml/1 tbsp single cream

30 ml/2 tbsp salad cream

15 ml/1 tbsp mayonnaise

5 ml/1 tsp prepared mild mustard

7.5 ml/1½ tsp sugar

salt

snipped fresh chives, to garnish

1 Peel the potatoes. Boil in salted water for 10–12 minutes, until tender. Drain and cool, then cut into cubes and place in a large mixing bowl.

2 Halve the peppers, cut away and discard the core and seeds and cut the flesh into small pieces. Finely chop the celery, shallot and spring onions and slice the chilli very thinly, discarding the seeds. Add the vegetables to the potatoes together with the garlic and herbs.

3 Blend the cream, salad cream, mayonnaise, mustard and sugar in a small bowl, stirring until the mixture is well combined.

4 Pour the dressing over the salad and stir gently to coat evenly. Serve, garnished with the snipped chives.

Potato Salad with Garlic Sausage

In this delicious potato salad, the potatoes are moistened with a little white wine before adding the vinaigrette.

INGREDIENTS

Serves 4

450 g/1 lb small waxy potatoes
30–45 ml/2–3 tbsp dry white wine
2 shallots, finely chopped
15 ml/1 tbsp chopped fresh parsley
15 ml/1 tbsp chopped fresh tarragon
175 g/6 oz cooked garlic sausage
fresh flat-leaf parsley sprig, to garnish

For the vinaigrette

10 ml/2 tsp Dijon mustard
15 ml/1 tbsp tarragon vinegar or white
    wine vinegar
75 ml/5 tbsp extra-virgin olive oil
salt and ground black pepper

1 Scrub the potatoes. Boil in salted water for 10–12 minutes, until tender. Drain and refresh under cold running water.

2 Peel the potatoes if you like, or leave in their skins, and cut into 5 mm/¼ in slices. Sprinkle with the wine and shallots.

VARIATION

The potatoes are also delicious served on their own, simply dressed with vinaigrette, and perhaps accompanied by marinated herrings.

3 To make the vinaigrette, mix the mustard and vinegar in a small bowl, then whisk in the oil, 15 ml/1 tbsp at a time. Season and pour over the potatoes.

4 Add the herbs to the potatoes and toss until well mixed.

5 Slice the garlic sausage thinly and toss with the potatoes. Season the salad with salt and pepper to taste and serve at room temperature, garnished with a sprig of parsley.

Peppery Bean Salad

This pretty salad uses canned beans for speed and convenience.

INGREDIENTS

Serves 4–6

425 g/15 oz can red kidney beans

425 g/15 oz can black-eyed beans

425 g/15 oz can chick-peas

¼ red pepper

¼ green pepper

6 radishes

15 ml/1 tbsp chopped spring onion

For the dressing

5 ml/1 tsp ground cumin

15 ml/1 tbsp tomato ketchup

30 ml/2 tbsp olive oil

15 ml/1 tbsp white wine vinegar

1 garlic clove, crushed

2.5 ml/½ tsp hot pepper sauce

1 Drain the red kidney beans, black-eyed beans and chick-peas and rinse under cold running water. Shake off the excess water and tip them into a large bowl.

2 Core, seed and chop the red and green peppers. Trim the radishes and slice thinly. Add the peppers, radishes and spring onion to the beans.

3 Mix together the cumin, ketchup, oil, vinegar and garlic in a small bowl. Add a little salt and hot pepper sauce to taste and stir again thoroughly.

4 Pour the dressing over the salad and mix. Chill the salad for at least 1 hour before serving, garnished with the sliced spring onion.

Smoked Ham and Bean Salad

A fairly substantial salad that should be served in small quantities if intended as an accompaniment.

INGREDIENTS

Serves 8

175 g/6 oz black-eyed beans

1 onion

1 carrot

225 g/8 oz smoked ham, diced

3 medium tomatoes, peeled, seeded and diced

salt and ground black pepper

For the dressing

2 garlic cloves, crushed

45 ml/3 tbsp olive oil

45 ml/3 tbsp red wine vinegar

30 ml/2 tbsp vegetable oil

15 ml/1 tbsp lemon juice

15 ml/1 tbsp chopped fresh or 5 ml/1 tsp dried basil

15 ml/1 tbsp wholegrain mustard

5 ml/1 tsp soy sauce

2.5 ml/½ tsp dried oregano

2.5 ml/½ tsp caster sugar

1.5 ml/¼ tsp Worcestershire sauce

2.5 ml/½ tsp chilli sauce

1 Soak the beans in cold water to cover overnight. Drain.

2 Put the beans in a large saucepan and add the onion and carrot. Cover with fresh cold water and bring to the boil. Lower the heat and simmer for about 1 hour, until the beans are tender.

3 Drain the beans, reserving the onion and carrot. Transfer the beans to a salad bowl.

4 Finely chop the onion and carrot. Toss with the beans. Stir in the ham and tomatoes.

5 For the dressing, combine all the ingredients in a small bowl and whisk to mix.

6 Pour the dressing over the ham and beans. Season with salt and pepper. Toss to combine, then serve.

White Bean and Celery Salad

This simple bean salad is a delicious alternative to the potato salad that seems to appear on every salad menu. If you do not have time to soak and cook dried beans, you can use canned ones.

INGREDIENTS

Serves 4

450 g/1 lb dried white beans (haricot, canellini, navy or butter beans) or

3 x 400 g/14 oz cans white beans

1 litre/1¾ pints/4 cups vegetable stock

3 celery sticks, cut into 1 cm/½ in strips

120 ml/4 fl oz/½ cup French Dressing

45 ml/3 tbsp chopped fresh parsley

salt and ground black pepper

1 If you are using dried beans, cover them with plenty of cold water and soak for at least 4 hours. Discard the soaking water, then place the beans in a heavy saucepan. Cover with water.

3 Place the cooked beans in a large saucepan. Add the vegetable stock and celery, bring to the boil, cover and simmer for 15 minutes. Drain thoroughly. Moisten the beans with the French dressing and leave to cool.

4 Add the chopped parsley and mix. Season to taste with salt and pepper, transfer to a salad bowl and serve.

2 Bring to the boil and simmer without a lid for 1½ hours, or until the skins are broken. Cooked beans will squash readily between a thumb and forefinger. Drain the beans. If using canned beans, drain and rinse.

Lentil and Cabbage Salad

A warm, crunchy salad that makes a satisfying meal if served with crusty French bread or wholemeal rolls.

INGREDIENTS

Serves 4–6

225 g/8 oz/1 cup puy lentils

3 garlic cloves

1 bay leaf

1 small onion, peeled and studded with 2 cloves

15 ml/1 tbsp olive oil

1 red onion, finely sliced

15 ml/1 tbsp fresh thyme leaves

350 g/12 oz cabbage, finely shredded

finely grated rind and juice of 1 lemon

15 ml/1 tbsp raspberry vinegar

salt and ground black pepper

1 Rinse the lentils in cold water and place in a large pan with 1.5 litres/2½ pints/6¼ cups cold water, 1 of the garlic cloves, the bay leaf and clove-studded onion. Bring to the boil and cook for 10 minutes. Reduce the heat, cover and simmer gently for 15–20 minutes. Drain and discard the onion, garlic and bay leaf.

2 Crush the remaining garlic cloves. Heat the oil in a large pan. Add the red onion, crushed garlic and thyme and cook for 5 minutes, until softened.

3 Add the cabbage and cook for 3–5 minutes, until just cooked but still crunchy.

4 Stir in the cooked lentils, lemon rind and juice and the raspberry vinegar. Season to taste and serve warm.

Brown Bean Salad

Brown beans, sometimes called ful medames, are available from health-food shops and Middle Eastern grocery stores. Dried broad beans or black or red kidney beans make a good substitute.

INGREDIENTS

Serves 6

350 g/12 oz/1½ cups dried brown beans

3 fresh thyme sprigs

2 bay leaves

1 onion, halved

4 garlic cloves, crushed

7.5 ml/1½ tsp crushed cumin seeds

3 spring onions, finely chopped

90 ml/6 tbsp chopped fresh parsley

20 ml/4 tsp lemon juice

90 ml/6 tbsp olive oil

3 hard-boiled eggs, roughly chopped

1 pickled cucumber, roughly chopped

salt and ground black pepper

1 Put the beans in a bowl with plenty of cold water and leave to soak overnight. Drain, transfer to a saucepan and cover with fresh water. Bring to the boil and boil rapidly for 10 minutes.

2 Reduce the heat and add the thyme, bay leaves and onion. Simmer very gently for about 1 hour, until tender. Drain and discard the herbs and onion.

> ### COOK'S TIP
>
>
> The cooking time for dried beans can vary considerably. They may need only 45 minutes, or a lot longer.

3 Place the beans in a large bowl. Mix together the garlic, cumin seeds, spring onions, parsley, lemon juice and oil in a small bowl, and add a little salt and pepper. Pour over the beans and toss the ingredients lightly together.

4 Gently stir in the eggs and pickled cucumber. Transfer the salad to a serving dish and serve at once.

Cracked Wheat Salad

Fresh herbs, bursting with the flavours of summer, are essential for this salad. Dried herbs will not make a suitable substitute.

INGREDIENTS

Serves 4

225 g/8 oz/1⅓ cups cracked wheat

350 ml/12 fl oz/1½ cups vegetable stock

1 cinnamon stick

generous pinch of ground cumin

pinch of cayenne pepper

pinch of ground cloves

5 ml/1 tsp salt

10 mangetouts, topped and tailed

1 red and 1 yellow pepper, roasted, skinned, seeded and diced

2 plum tomatoes, peeled, seeded and diced

2 shallots, finely sliced

5 black olives, pitted and cut into quarters

30 ml/2 tbsp each shredded fresh basil, mint and parsley

30 ml/2 tbsp roughly chopped walnuts

30 ml/2 tbsp balsamic vinegar

120 ml/4 fl oz/½ cup extra-virgin olive oil

ground black pepper

onion rings, to garnish

1 Place the cracked wheat in a large bowl. Pour the stock into a saucepan and bring to the boil with the spices and salt.

2 Cook for 1 minute, then pour the stock, with the cinnamon stick, over the cracked wheat. Leave to stand for 30 minutes.

3 In another bowl, mix together the mangetouts, peppers, tomatoes, shallots, olives, herbs and walnuts. Add the vinegar, olive oil and a little black pepper and stir thoroughly to mix.

4 Strain the cracked wheat of any liquid and discard the cinnamon stick. Place the cracked wheat in a serving bowl, stir in the fresh vegetable mixture and serve, garnished with onion rings.

Fruity Brown Rice Salad

An oriental-style dressing accompanies this salad. Brown rice has a nuttier flavour than white rice.

INGREDIENTS

Serves 4–6

115 g/4 oz/⅔ cup brown rice

1 small red pepper, seeded and diced

200 g/7 oz can sweetcorn niblets, drained

45 ml/3 tbsp sultanas

225 g/8 oz can pineapple pieces in fruit juice

15 ml/1 tbsp light soy sauce

15 ml/1 tbsp sunflower oil

15 ml/1 tbsp hazelnut oil

1 garlic clove, crushed

5 ml/1 tsp finely chopped fresh root ginger

salt and ground black pepper

4 spring onions, sliced, to garnish

1 Cook the brown rice in a large saucepan of lightly salted boiling water for about 30 minutes, or until it is tender. Drain thoroughly and cool. Meanwhile, prepare the garnish. Slice the spring onions at an angle, as shown, then set aside.

2 Tip the rice into a large serving bowl and add the red pepper, sweetcorn and sultanas. Drain the pineapple pieces, reserving the juice, then add them to the rice mixture and toss lightly.

3 Pour the reserved pineapple juice into a clean screw-top jar. Add the soy sauce, sunflower and hazelnut oils, garlic and root ginger. Season with salt and pepper. Close the jar tightly and shake well to combine.

4 Pour the dressing over the salad and toss well. Scatter the spring onions over the top and serve.

COOK'S TIP

Hazelnut oil gives a wonderfully distinctive flavour to any salad dressing. Like olive oil, it contains mainly mono-unsaturated fats.

Couscous Salad

There are many ways of serving couscous. This salad has a delicate flavour and is excellent with grilled chicken or kebabs.

INGREDIENTS

Serves 4

275 g/10 oz/1²⁄₃ cups couscous

550 ml/18 fl oz/2¹⁄₄ cups boiling
   vegetable stock

16–20 black olives

2 small courgettes

25 g/1 oz/¹⁄₄ cup flaked almonds, toasted

60 ml/4 tbsp olive oil

15 ml/1 tbsp lemon juice

15 ml/1 tbsp chopped fresh coriander

15 ml/1 tbsp chopped fresh parsley

good pinch of ground cumin

good pinch of cayenne pepper

salt

3 Carefully mix the courgettes, olives and toasted almonds into the couscous.

4 Mix together the olive oil, lemon juice, herbs, spices and a pinch of salt in a small jug or bowl. Stir into the salad.

1 Place the couscous in a bowl and pour over the boiling stock. Stir with a fork and then set aside for 10 minutes for the stock to be absorbed. Fluff up with a fork.

2 Halve the olives, discarding the stones. Top and tail the courgettes and cut them into small julienne strips.

Orange and Cracked Wheat Salad

Cracked wheat makes an excellent alternative to rice or pasta as a filling side salad.

INGREDIENTS

Serves 4

1 small green pepper
150 g/5 oz/scant 1 cup cracked wheat
¼ cucumber, diced
15 g/½ oz/½ cup chopped fresh mint
40 g/1½ oz/⅓ cup flaked almonds, toasted
grated rind and juice of 1 lemon
2 seedless oranges, peeled
salt and ground black pepper
fresh mint sprigs, to garnish

1 Using a sharp vegetable knife, carefully halve and seed the green pepper. Cut into small cubes and put to one side.

2 Place the cracked wheat in a saucepan and add 600 ml/ 1 pint/2½ cups water. Bring to the boil, lower the heat, cover and simmer for 10–15 minutes, until tender. Alternatively, place the cracked wheat in a heatproof bowl, pour over boiling water and leave to soak for 30 minutes. Most, if not all, of the water should be absorbed; drain off any excess.

3 Toss the cracked wheat with the cucumber, green pepper, mint and toasted almonds in a serving bowl. Add the grated lemon rind and juice.

4 Working over the salad bowl to catch the juice, cut the oranges into neat segments, leaving the membrane behind. Add the segments to the cracked wheat mixture, then season with salt and pepper and toss lightly. Garnish with mint sprigs and serve.

VARIATION
CRACKED WHEAT SALAD WITH FENNEL AND POMEGRANATE

This version uses the added crunchiness of fennel and the sweetness of pomegranate seeds. Perfect for a summer lunch.

INGREDIENTS

Serves 6

225 g/8 oz/1⅓ cups cracked wheat
2 fennel bulbs
1 small red chilli, seeded and finely chopped
1 celery stick, finely sliced
30 ml/2 tbsp olive oil
finely grated rind and juice of 2 lemons
6–8 spring onions, chopped
90 ml/6 tbsp chopped fresh mint
90 ml/6 tbsp chopped fresh parsley
the seeds from 1 pomegranate
salt and ground black pepper
lettuce leaves, to serve

1 Place the cracked wheat in a bowl and pour over enough boiling water to cover. Leave to stand for 30 minutes.

2 Drain through a sieve, pressing out excess water.

3 Halve the fennel bulbs and cut into very fine slices.

4 Mix all the remaining ingredients together, then stir in the cracked wheat and fennel. Season well, cover and set aside for 30 minutes before serving with lettuce leaves.

MAIN COURSE
SALADS

Salade Niçoise

Served with good French bread, this regional classic makes a wonderful summer lunch or light supper dish.

INGREDIENTS

Serves 4–6

225 g/8 oz French beans

450 g/1 lb new potatoes, peeled and cut into 2.5 cm/1 in pieces

white wine vinegar and olive oil, for sprinkling

1 small cos or round lettuce, torn into bite-sized pieces

4 ripe plum tomatoes, quartered

1 small cucumber, peeled, seeded and diced

1 green or red pepper, seeded and thinly sliced

4 hard-boiled eggs, peeled and quartered

24 black olives

225 g/8 oz can tuna in brine, drained

50 g/2 oz can anchovy fillets in olive oil, drained

basil leaves, to garnish

garlic croûtons, to serve

For the anchovy vinaigrette

20 ml/4 tsp Dijon mustard

50 g/2 oz can anchovy fillets in olive oil, drained

1 garlic clove, crushed

60 ml/4 tbsp lemon juice or white wine vinegar

120 ml/4 fl oz/¹/₂ cup sunflower oil

120 ml/4 fl oz/¹/₂ cup extra-virgin olive oil

ground black pepper

1 First make the anchovy vinaigrette. Place the mustard, anchovies and garlic in a bowl and mix together by pressing the garlic and anchovies against the sides of the bowl. Season generously with pepper. Using a small whisk, blend in the lemon juice or vinegar. Slowly whisk in the sunflower oil in a thin stream, followed by the olive oil, whisking until the dressing is smooth and creamy.

2 Alternatively, put all the ingredients except the oils in a food processor fitted with the metal blade and process to combine. With the machine running, slowly add the oils in a thin stream until the vinaigrette is thick and creamy.

3 Drop the French beans into a large saucepan of boiling water and boil for 3 minutes until tender, yet crisp. Transfer the beans to a colander with a slotted spoon, then rinse under cold running water. Drain again and set aside.

4 Add the potatoes to the same boiling water, reduce the heat and simmer for 10–15 minutes, until just tender, then drain. Sprinkle with a little vinegar and olive oil and a spoonful of the vinaigrette.

5 Arrange the lettuce on a serving platter, top with the tomatoes, cucumber and red or green pepper, then add the French beans and potatoes.

6 Arrange the eggs around the edge. Place olives, tuna and anchovies on top and garnish with the basil leaves. Drizzle with the remaining vinaigrette and serve with garlic croûtons.

COOK'S TIP
∾

To make garlic croûtons, thinly slice a French stick or cut a larger loaf, such as rustic country bread, into 2.5 cm/1 in cubes. Place the bread in a single layer on a baking sheet and cook in the oven, preheated to 180°C/350°F/Gas 4, for 7–10 minutes or until golden, turning once. Rub the toast with a garlic clove and serve hot, or allow to cool and store in an airtight container.

Moroccan Tuna Salad

This salad is similar to the classic Salade Niçoise but uses tuna or swordfish steaks and fresh broad beans along with the familiar French beans.

INGREDIENTS

Serves 6

about 900 g/2 lb fresh tuna or swordfish, sliced into 2 cm/³⁄₄ in steaks
olive oil, for brushing

For the salad

450 g/1 lb French beans, topped and tailed
450 g/1 lb broad beans
1 cos lettuce
450 g/1 lb cherry tomatoes, halved, unless very tiny
30 ml/2 tbsp coarsely chopped fresh coriander
3 hard-boiled eggs
45 ml/3 tbsp olive oil
10–15 ml/2–3 tsp lime or lemon juice
¹⁄₂ garlic clove, crushed
175–225 g/6–8 oz/1¹⁄₂–2 cups pitted black olives

For the marinade

1 onion
2 garlic cloves
¹⁄₂ bunch fresh parsley
¹⁄₂ bunch fresh coriander
10 ml/2 tsp paprika
45 ml/3 tbsp olive oil
30 ml/2 tbsp white wine vinegar
15 ml/1 tbsp lime or lemon juice

1 First make the marinade. Place all the ingredients in a food processor, add 45 ml/3 tbsp water and process for 30–40 seconds, until finely chopped.

2 Prick the tuna or swordfish steaks all over with a fork, place in a shallow dish and pour over the marinade, turning the fish so that each piece is well coated. Cover with clear film and leave in a cool place for 2–4 hours.

3 To prepare the salad, cook the French beans and broad beans in boiling salted water until tender. Drain and refresh under cold water. Discard the outer shells from the broad beans and place in a large serving bowl with the French beans.

4 Discard the outer lettuce leaves and tear the inner leaves into pieces. Add to the salad with the tomatoes and coriander. Shell the eggs and cut into eighths. Mix the olive oil, lime or lemon juice and garlic to make a dressing.

5 Preheat the grill and arrange the tuna or swordfish steaks in a grill pan. Brush with the marinade together with a little extra olive oil and grill for 5–6 minutes on each side, until the fish is tender and flakes easily. Brush with marinade and more olive oil when turning the fish over.

6 Allow the fish to cool a little then break the steaks into large pieces. Toss into the salad with the olives and the dressing. Decorate with the eggs and serve.

Warm Fish Salad with Mango Dressing

This salad is best served during the summer months, preferably out of doors. The dressing combines the flavour of rich mango with hot chilli, ginger and lime.

INGREDIENTS

Serves 4

1 French loaf

4 redfish, black bream or porgy, each about 275 g/10 oz

15 ml/1 tbsp vegetable oil

1 mango

1 cm/½ in fresh root ginger

1 red chilli, seeded and finely chopped

30 ml/2 tbsp lime juice

30 ml/2 tbsp chopped fresh coriander

175 g/6 oz young spinach

150 g/5 oz pak choi

175 g/6 oz cherry tomatoes, halved

1 Preheat the oven to 180°C/ 350°F/Gas 4. Cut the French loaf into 20 cm/8 in lengths. Slice lengthways, then cut into thick fingers. Place the bread on a baking sheet and leave to dry in the oven for 15 minutes.

2 Preheat the grill or light the barbecue and allow the embers to settle. Slash the fish deeply on both sides and moisten with oil. Grill or barbecue the fish for 6 minutes, turning once.

3 Peel the mango and cut in half, discarding the stone. Thinly slice one half and set aside. Place the other half in a food processor. Peel the ginger, grate finely, then add to the mango with the chilli, lime juice and coriander. Process until smooth. Adjust to a pouring consistency with 30–45 ml/ 2–3 tbsp water.

4 Wash the spinach and pak choi leaves and spin dry, then distribute them among four serving plates. Place the fish over the leaves. Spoon on the mango dressing and finish with the reserved slices of mango and the tomato halves. Serve with the fingers of crispy French bread.

Grilled Salmon and Spring Vegetable Salad

Spring is the time to enjoy sweet, young vegetables. Cook them briefly, cool to room temperature, dress and serve with a piece of lightly grilled salmon topped with sorrel and quail's eggs.

INGREDIENTS

Serves 4

350 g/12 oz small new potatoes, scrubbed or scraped

4 quail's eggs

115 g/4 oz young carrots, peeled

115 g/4 oz baby sweetcorn

115 g/4 oz sugar snap peas, topped and tailed

115 g/4 oz fine green beans, topped and tailed

115 g/4 oz young courgettes

115 g/4 oz patty-pan squash (optional)

120 ml/4 fl oz/½ cup French Dressing

4 salmon fillets, each about 150 g/5 oz, skinned

115 g/4 oz sorrel, stems removed

salt and ground black pepper

1 Bring the potatoes to the boil in salted water and cook for about 15 minutes, until tender. Drain, cover and keep warm.

2 Cover the quail's eggs with boiling water and cook for 8 minutes. Refresh under cold water, shell and cut in half.

3 Bring a saucepan of salted water to the boil, add the carrots, sweetcorn, sugar snap peas, beans, courgettes and squash, if using, and cook for 2–3 minutes. Drain well. Place the hot vegetables and potatoes in a bowl, moisten with a little French Dressing and allow to cool.

4 Brush the salmon fillets with some of the French Dressing and grill for 6 minutes, turning once.

5 Place the sorrel in a stainless-steel or enamel saucepan with 30 ml/2 tbsp French Dressing. Cover and soften over a gentle heat for 2 minutes. Strain in a small sieve and cool to room temperature.

6 Divide the potatoes and vegetables between four large serving plates, then position a piece of salmon to one side of each plate. Place a spoonful of sorrel on each piece of salmon and top with two pieces of quail's egg. Season and serve at room temperature.

VARIATION

If sorrel is unavailable, use young spinach leaves instead. Cook it gently in the same way as the sorrel.

Noodles with Pineapple, Ginger and Chillies

A coconut, lime and fish sauce dressing is the perfect partner to this fruity and spicy salad.

Serves 4

275 g/10 oz dried udon noodles

½ pineapple, peeled, cored and sliced into 4 cm/1½ in rings

45 ml/3 tbsp soft light brown sugar

60 ml/4 tbsp lime juice

60 ml/4 tbsp coconut milk

30 ml/2 tbsp Thai fish sauce

30 ml/2 tbsp grated fresh root ginger

2 garlic cloves, finely chopped

1 ripe mango or 2 peaches, finely diced

ground black pepper

2 spring onions, finely sliced, 2 red chillies, seeded and finely shredded, and fresh mint leaves, to garnish

1 Cook the noodles in a large saucepan of boiling water until tender, following the directions on the packet. Drain, refresh under cold water and drain again.

2 Place the pineapple rings in a flameproof dish, sprinkle with 30 ml/2 tbsp of the sugar and grill for about 5 minutes, or until golden. Cool slightly and cut into small dice.

3 Mix the lime juice, coconut milk and fish sauce in a salad bowl. Add the remaining brown sugar with the ginger, garlic and black pepper and whisk well. Add the noodles and pineapple.

4 Add the mango or peaches and toss. Scatter over the spring onions, chillies and mint leaves before serving.

Buckwheat Noodles with Smoked Salmon

Young pea sprouts are available for only a short time. You can substitute watercress, salad cress, young leeks or your favourite green vegetable or herb in this dish.

Serves 4

225 g/8 oz buckwheat or soba noodles

15 ml/1 tbsp oyster sauce

juice of ½ lemon

30–45 ml/2–3 tbsp light olive oil

115 g/4 oz smoked salmon, cut into fine strips

115 g/4 oz young pea sprouts

2 ripe tomatoes, peeled, seeded and cut into strips

15 ml/1 tbsp snipped chives

ground black pepper

1 Cook the buckwheat or soba noodles in a large saucepan of boiling water until tender, following the directions on the packet. Drain, then rinse under cold running water and drain well.

2 Tip the noodles into a large bowl. Add the oyster sauce and lemon juice and season with pepper to taste. Moisten the noodles with the olive oil.

3 Add the smoked salmon, pea sprouts, tomatoes and chives. Mix well and serve at once.

Smoked Trout and Noodle Salad

It is important to use ripe, juicy tomatoes for this fresh-tasting salad. For a special occasion you could use smoked salmon.

INGREDIENTS

Serves 4

225 g/8 oz somen noodles
2 smoked trout, skinned and boned
2 hard-boiled eggs, coarsely chopped
30 ml/2 tbsp snipped fresh chives
lime halves, to serve (optional)

For the dressing
6 ripe plum tomatoes
2 shallots, finely chopped
30 ml/2 tbsp tiny capers, rinsed
30 ml/2 tbsp chopped fresh tarragon
finely grated rind and juice of ½ orange
60 ml/4 tbsp extra-virgin olive oil
salt and ground black pepper

1 To make the dressing, cut the tomatoes in half, remove the cores and cut the flesh into chunks.

2 Place in a bowl with the shallots, capers, tarragon, orange rind and juice and olive oil. Season with salt and pepper and mix well. Leave to marinate at room temperature for 1–2 hours.

3 Cook the noodles in a large saucepan of boiling water, following the directions on the packet, until just tender. Drain and rinse under cold running water. Drain well.

4 Toss the noodles with the dressing, then adjust the seasoning to taste. Arrange the noodles on a large serving platter or individual plates.

5 Flake the smoked trout over the noodles, then sprinkle the eggs and chives over the top. Serve, with lime halves on the side of the plate, if you like.

Smoked Trout and Horseradish Salad

In the summer, when lettuce leaves are sweet and crisp, partner them with fillets of smoked trout, warm new potatoes and a creamy horseradish dressing.

INGREDIENTS

Serves 4

675 g/1½ lb new potatoes

4 smoked trout fillets

115 g/4 oz mixed lettuce leaves

4 slices dark rye bread, cut into fingers

salt and ground black pepper

For the dressing

60 ml/4 tbsp creamed horseradish

60 ml/4 tbsp groundnut oil

15 ml/1 tbsp white wine vinegar

10 ml/2 tsp caraway seeds

1 Scrub the potatoes. Bring to the boil in a saucepan of salted water and simmer for about 15 minutes, until tender. Remove the skin from the trout fillets and lift the flesh from the bone.

COOK'S TIP

In some cases it is better to season the leaves rather than the dressing when making a salad.

2 To make the dressing, place all the ingredients in a screw-top jar and shake vigorously. Season the lettuce leaves and moisten them with the dressing. Distribute between four serving plates.

3 Flake the trout fillets and cut the potatoes in half. Scatter them together with the rye bread fingers over the salad leaves and toss to mix. Season the salad to taste and serve.

Prawn and Artichoke Salad

The mild flavours of prawns and artichoke hearts are complemented by a zingy herb dressing.

INGREDIENTS

Serves 4

1 garlic clove

10 ml/2 tsp Dijon mustard

60 ml/4 tbsp red wine vinegar

150 ml/¼ pint/⅔ cup olive oil

45 ml/3 tbsp shredded fresh basil leaves or 30 ml/2 tbsp finely chopped fresh parsley

1 red onion, very finely sliced

350 g/12 oz shelled cooked prawns

400 g/14 oz can artichoke hearts

½ iceberg lettuce

salt and ground black pepper

1 Chop the garlic, then crush it to a pulp with 5 ml/1 tsp salt, using the flat edge of a heavy knife blade. Mix the garlic and mustard to a paste in a small bowl.

2 Beat in the vinegar and finally the olive oil, beating hard to make a thick, creamy dressing. Season with black pepper and, if necessary, additional salt.

3 Stir the basil or parsley into the dressing, followed by the sliced onion. Leave to stand for 30 minutes at room temperature, then stir in the prawns and refrigerate for 1 hour, or until ready to serve.

4 Drain the artichoke hearts and halve each one. Shred the lettuce finely.

5 Make a bed of lettuce on a serving platter or four individual salad plates and spread the artichoke hearts over it.

6 Immediately before serving, pour the prawns and their marinade over the top of the salad.

Ghanaian Prawn Salad

The addition of plantain, which is first cooked in its skin, brings an unusual flavour to this salad.

INGREDIENTS

Serves 4

115 g/4 oz cooked shelled prawns

1 garlic clove, crushed

7.5 ml/1½ tsp vegetable oil

2 eggs

1 yellow plantain, halved

4 lettuce leaves

2 tomatoes

1 red pepper, seeded

1 avocado

juice of 1 lemon

1 carrot

200 g/7 oz can tuna or sardines, drained

1 green chilli, finely chopped

30 ml/2 tbsp chopped spring onion

salt and ground black pepper

1 Put the prawns and garlic in a small bowl. Add a little seasoning.

2 Heat the oil in a small saucepan, add the prawns and cook over a low heat for a few minutes. Transfer to a plate to cool.

VARIATION

To vary this salad, use other types of canned fish and a mixture of interesting lettuce leaves.

3 Hard-boil the eggs, place in cold water to cool, then shell and cut into slices.

4 Boil the unpeeled plantain in a pan of water for 15 minutes, cool, then peel and cut into thick slices.

5 Shred the lettuce and arrange on a large serving plate. Slice the tomatoes and red pepper and peel and slice the avocado, sprinkling it with a little lemon juice.

6 Cut the carrot into matchstick-size pieces and arrange over the lettuce with the other vegetables.

7 Add the plantain, eggs, prawns and tuna or sardines. Sprinkle with the remaining lemon juice, scatter the chilli and spring onion on top, season and serve.

Prawn Salad with Curry Dressing

Curry spices add an unexpected twist to this salad. The warm flavours combine especially well with the sweet prawns and grated apple. Curry paste is needed here rather than curry powder as there is no cooking, which is necessary for bringing out the flavours of powdered spices.

INGREDIENTS

Serves 4

1 ripe tomato

½ iceberg lettuce

1 small onion

1 small bunch fresh coriander

15 ml/1 tbsp lemon juice

450 g/1 lb shelled cooked prawns

1 apple

8 whole prawns, 8 lemon wedges and
    4 fresh coriander sprigs, to garnish

salt

For the curry dressing

75 ml/5 tbsp mayonnaise

5 ml/1 tsp mild curry paste

15 ml/1 tbsp tomato ketchup

sake

1 To peel the tomato, cut a cross in the skin with a knife and immerse in boiling water for 30 seconds. Drain and cool under running water. Peel off the skin. Halve the tomato, push the seeds out with your thumb and discard them. Cut the flesh into large dice.

2 Finely shred the lettuce and put in a large bowl, then finely chop the onion and coriander. Add to the bowl together with the tomato, moisten with lemon juice and season with salt.

3 To make the dressing, combine the mayonnaise, curry paste and tomato ketchup in a small bowl. Add 30 ml/2 tbsp water to thin the dressing and season to taste with salt.

COOK'S TIP

Fresh coriander is inclined to wilt if it is kept out of water. Put it in a jar of water, cover with a plastic bag and place in the fridge and it will stay fresh for several days.

4 Combine the prawns with the dressing and stir gently so that all the prawns are coated with the dressing.

5 Quarter and core the apple and grate into the prawn and dressing mixture.

6 Distribute the shredded lettuce mixture among four serving plates or bowls. Pile the prawn mixture in the centre of each and decorate each with two whole prawns, two lemon wedges and a sprig of coriander.

Prawn and Mint Salad

Fresh, uncooked prawns make all the difference to this salad as cooking them in butter adds to the piquant flavour. Garnish with shavings of fresh coconut for a tropical topping, if you wish.

INGREDIENTS

Serves 4

12 large fresh, uncooked prawns
15 ml/1 tbsp unsalted butter
15 ml/1 tbsp Thai fish sauce
juice of 1 lime
45 ml/3 tbsp thin coconut milk
5 ml/1 tsp caster sugar
1 garlic clove, crushed
2.5 cm/1 in fresh root ginger, peeled
  and grated
2 red chillies, seeded and finely chopped
30 ml/2 tbsp fresh mint leaves
225 g/8 oz light green lettuce leaves
ground black pepper

1 Carefully peel the uncooked prawns, removing and discarding the heads and outer shells, but leaving the tails intact.

2 Using a sharp knife, carefully remove the dark-coloured vein that runs along the back of each prawn.

3 Melt the butter in a large frying pan. When the melted butter is foaming add the prawns and toss on a high heat until they turn pink. Remove from the heat, it is important not to cook them for too long so that their tenderness is retained.

4 In a small bowl mix the fish sauce, lime juice, coconut milk, sugar, garlic, ginger and chillies together. Season to taste with freshly ground black pepper.

5 Toss the warm prawns into the sauce with the mint leaves. Arrange the lettuce leaves on a serving plate and place the prawn and mint mixture in the centre.

VARIATION

Instead of prawns, this dish also works very well with lobster tails if you are feeling very extravagant.

COOK'S TIP

If you can't find any fresh, uncooked prawns you could use frozen ones. To make the most of their flavour, toss very quickly in the hot butter when they are completely thawed.

Mixed Seafood Salad

Use fresh seafood that is in season, or you can use a combination of fresh and frozen seafood.

INGREDIENTS

Serves 6–8

350 g/12 oz small squid

1 small onion, cut into quarters

1 bay leaf

200 g/7 oz uncooked prawns, in
   their shells

750 g/1½ lb fresh mussels, in their shells

450 g/1 lb fresh small clams

175 ml/6 fl oz/¾ cup white wine

1 fennel bulb

For the dressing

75 ml/5 tbsp extra-virgin olive oil

45 ml/3 tbsp lemon juice

1 garlic clove, finely chopped

salt and ground black pepper

1 Working near the sink, clean the squid by first peeling off the thin skin from the body section. Rinse well.

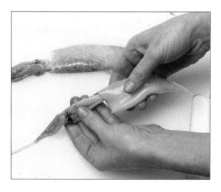

2 Pull the head and tentacles away from the sac section. Remove and discard the translucent quill and any remaining insides from the sac. Sever the tentacles and head.

3 Discard the head and intestines. Remove the small, hard beak from the base of the tentacles. Rinse the sac and tentacles under cold water. Drain.

4 Bring a large pan of water to the boil. Add the onion and bay leaf. Drop in the squid and cook for about 10 minutes, or until tender. Remove with a slotted spoon and allow to cool before slicing into rings 1 cm/½ in wide. Cut each tentacle section into two pieces. Set aside.

5 Drop the prawns into the same boiling water and cook for about 2 minutes, until they turn pink. Remove with a slotted spoon. Shell and de-vein. (The cooking liquid may be strained and kept for soup.)

6 Cut the "beards" from the mussels. Scrub and rinse the mussels and clams well in several changes of cold water. Any that are open should close if given a sharp tap; if they fail to do so, discard. Place in a large saucepan with the wine. Cover and steam until all the shells have opened. (Discard any that do not open.) Lift the clams and mussels out of the pan.

7 Remove all the clams from their shells with a small spoon. Place in a large serving bowl. Remove all but eight of the mussels from their shells and add them to the clams in the bowl. Leave the remaining mussels in their half-shells, and set aside.

8 Cut the green, ferny part of the fennel away from the bulb. Chop finely and set aside. Chop the bulb into bite-size pieces and add it to the serving bowl together with the squid and prawns.

9 To make the dressing, combine the oil, lemon juice and garlic in a bowl. Add the reserved chopped fennel green and salt and pepper to taste. Pour over the salad, and toss well. Decorate with the remaining mussels in their half-shelves. Serve at room temperature or lightly chilled.

Avocado, Crab and Coriander Salad

*The sweet richness of crab combines
especially well with ripe avocado,
fresh coriander and tomato.*

INGREDIENTS

Serves 4

675 g/1½ lb small new potatoes

1 fresh mint sprig

900 g/2 lb boiled crabs or 275 g/10 oz
    frozen crab meat

1 endive or butterhead lettuce

175 g/6 oz lamb's lettuce or young
    spinach leaves

1 large ripe avocado, peeled and sliced

175 g/6 oz cherry tomatoes

salt, ground black pepper and freshly
    grated nutmeg

For the dressing

75 ml/5 tbsp olive oil

15 ml/1 tbsp lime juice

45 ml/3 tbsp chopped fresh coriander

2.5 ml/½ tsp caster sugar

1 Scrape or peel the potatoes.
Cover with water, add a good
pinch of salt and a sprig of mint.
Bring to the boil and simmer for
about 15 minutes, until tender.
Drain the potatoes, cover and keep
warm until needed.

2 Remove the legs and claws
from each crab. Crack these
open with the back of a chopping
knife and remove the white meat.

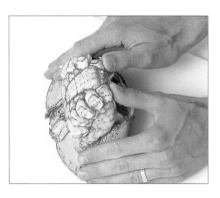

3 Turn the crab on its back and
push the rear leg section away
with the thumb and forefinger of
each hand. Remove the flesh from
inside the shell.

4 Discard the "dead men's
fingers", the soft gills which
the crab uses to filter impurities in
its diet. Apart from these and the
shell, everything else is edible, both
white and dark meat.

5 Split the central body section
open with a knife and remove
the white and dark flesh with a
pick or skewer.

6 Combine all the dressing
ingredients in a screw-top jar
and shake. Put the salad leaves in a
large bowl, pour the dressing over
and toss well.

7 Distribute the leaves among
four serving plates. Top with
the avocado, crab, tomatoes and
warm new potatoes. Season with
salt, pepper and freshly grated
nutmeg and serve.

COOK'S TIP

Young crabs offer the sweetest
meat, but are more fiddly to
prepare than older, larger ones.
The hen crab carries more flesh
than the cock which is
considered to have a better
overall flavour. The cock crab,
shown here, is identified by his
narrow apron flap at the rear.
    The hen has a broad flap,
under which she carries her eggs.
    Frozen crab meat is a good
alternative to fresh and retains
much of its original sweetness.

Thai Noodle Salad

The addition of coconut milk and sesame oil gives an unusual nutty flavour to the dressing for this colourful noodle salad.

INGREDIENTS

Serves 4–6

350 g/12 oz somen noodles

1 large carrot, cut into thin strips

1 bunch asparagus, trimmed and cut into
4 cm/1½ in lengths

1 red pepper, seeded and cut into
fine strips

115 g/4 oz mangetouts, topped, tailed
and halved

115 g/4 oz baby corn cobs, halved
lengthways

115 g/4 oz beansprouts

115 g/4 oz can water chestnuts, drained
and finely sliced

1 lime, cut into wedges, 50 g/2 oz/½ cup
roasted peanuts, roughly chopped, and
fresh coriander leaves, to garnish

For the dressing

45 ml/3 tbsp roughly torn fresh basil

75 ml/5 tbsp roughly chopped fresh mint

250 ml/8 fl oz/1 cup coconut milk

30 ml/2 tbsp dark sesame oil

15 ml/1 tbsp grated fresh root ginger

2 garlic cloves, finely chopped

juice of 1 lime

2 spring onions, finely chopped

salt and cayenne pepper

1 To make the dressing, combine all the ingredients in a bowl and mix well. Season to taste with salt and cayenne pepper.

2 Cook the noodles in a saucepan of boiling water, following the directions on the packet, until just tender. Drain, rinse under cold running water and drain again.

3 Cook all the vegetables, except the water chestnuts, in separate saucepans of boiling, lightly salted water until they are tender but still crisp. Drain, plunge them immediately into cold water and drain again.

4 Toss the noodles, vegetables, water chestnuts and dressing together. Arrange on individual serving plates and garnish with the lime wedges, chopped peanuts and coriander leaves.

Prawn Noodle Salad with Fragrant Herbs

A light, refreshing salad with all the tangy flavour of the sea. Instead of prawns, you can also use squid, scallops, mussels or crab.

INGREDIENTS

Serves 4

115 g/4 oz cellophane noodles, soaked in
   hot water until soft
1 small green pepper, seeded and cut
   into strips
½ cucumber, cut into strips
1 tomato, cut into strips
2 shallots, finely sliced
16 shelled cooked prawns
salt and ground black pepper
fresh coriander leaves, to garnish

For the dressing
15 ml/1 tbsp rice-wine vinegar
30 ml/2 tbsp Thai fish sauce
30 ml/2 tbsp lime juice
2.5 ml/½ tsp grated fresh root ginger
1 lemon grass stalk, finely chopped
1 red chilli, seeded and finely sliced
30 ml/2 tbsp roughly chopped fresh mint
few sprigs of tarragon, roughly chopped
15 ml/1 tbsp snipped fresh chives
pinch of salt

1 To make the dressing, combine all the ingredients in a small bowl or jug and whisk well.

2 Drain the noodles, then plunge them in a saucepan of boiling water for 1 minute. Drain, rinse under cold running water and drain again well.

3 In a large bowl, combine the noodles with the green pepper, cucumber, tomato and shallots. Lightly season with salt and pepper, then toss with the dressing.

COOK'S TIP

Prawns are available ready-cooked and often shelled. To cook prawns, boil them for 5 minutes. Leave them to cool in the cooking liquid, then gently pull off the tail shell and twist off the head.

4 Spoon the noodles on to individual serving plates, arranging the prawns on top. Garnish with a few coriander leaves and serve at once.

Egg Noodle Salad with Sesame Chicken

Quickly stir-fried chicken is served warm in a nest of crunchy salad vegetables and noodles.

INGREDIENTS

Serves 4–6

400 g/14 oz fresh thin egg noodles

1 carrot, cut into long fine strips

50 g/2 oz mangetouts, topped, tailed, cut into fine strips and blanched

115 g/4 oz/½ cup beansprouts, blanched

30 ml/2 tbsp olive oil

225 g/8 oz skinless, boneless chicken breast, finely sliced

30 ml/2 tbsp sesame seeds, toasted

2 spring onions, finely sliced diagonally, and fresh coriander leaves, to garnish

For the dressing

45 ml/3 tbsp sherry vinegar

75 ml/5 tbsp soy sauce

60 ml/4 tbsp sesame oil

90 ml/6 tbsp light olive oil

1 garlic clove, finely chopped

5 ml/1 tsp grated fresh root ginger

salt and ground black pepper

1 To make the dressing, whisk together all the ingredients in a small bowl. Season to taste.

2 Cook the noodles in a large saucepan of boiling water. Stir them occasionally to separate. They will take only a few minutes to cook; be careful not to overcook them. Drain the noodles, rinse under cold running water and drain well. Tip into a bowl.

3 Add the carrot, mangetouts and beansprouts to the noodles. Pour in about half the dressing, then toss the mixture well and adjust the seasoning according to taste.

4 Heat the oil in a large frying pan. Add the chicken and stir-fry for 3 minutes, or until cooked and golden. Remove from the heat. Add the sesame seeds and drizzle in some of the remaining dressing.

5 Arrange the noodle mixture on individual serving plates, making a nest on each plate. Spoon the chicken on top. Sprinkle with the spring onions and coriander leaves and serve any remaining dressing separately.

Chicken and Pasta Salad

This is a delicious way to use up left-over cooked chicken and, with the pasta, it makes a filling meal.

Serves 4

225 g/8 oz tri-coloured pasta twists

30 ml/2 tbsp bottled pesto sauce

15 ml/1 tbsp olive oil

1 beef tomato

12 pitted black olives

225 g/8 oz French beans, cooked

350 g/12 oz cooked chicken, cubed

salt and ground black pepper

fresh basil, to garnish

3 Peel the beef tomato by cutting a cross in the skin and plunging it in boiling water for about 30 seconds. The skin will now pull away easily. Cut the tomato into small cubes.

4 Add the tomato and olives to the pasta. Cut the French beans into 4 cm/1½ in lengths. Add the beans and chicken and season to taste. Toss gently, transfer to a serving platter, garnish with basil, and serve.

1 Cook the pasta in plenty of boiling, salted water until *al dente* (for about 12 minutes or as directed on the packet).

2 Drain the pasta and rinse in plenty of cold running water. Put into a bowl and stir in the pesto sauce and olive oil.

Corn-fed Chicken Salad with Garlic Bread

This makes a light first course for eight people or a substantial main course for four.

Serves 4

1.75 kg/4–4¹⁄₂ lb corn-fed chicken

300 ml/¹⁄₂ pint/1¹⁄₄ cups white wine and water, mixed

24 slices French bread, 5 mm/¹⁄₄ in thick

1 garlic clove, peeled

225 g/8 oz French beans

115 g/4 oz young spinach leaves

2 celery sticks, thinly sliced

2 sun-dried tomatoes, chopped

2 spring onions, thinly sliced

fresh chives and parsley, to garnish

For the vinaigrette

30 ml/2 tbsp red wine vinegar

90 ml/6 tbsp olive oil

15 ml/1 tbsp wholegrain mustard

15 ml/1 tbsp clear honey

30 ml/2 tbsp chopped fresh mixed herbs, such as thyme, parsley, chives

10 ml/2 tsp finely chopped capers

salt and ground black pepper

1 Preheat the oven to 190°C/ 375°F/Gas 5. Put the chicken into a casserole with the wine and water. Cook in the oven for 1¹⁄₂ hours, until tender. Leave to cool in the liquid. Discard the skin and bones and cut the flesh into small pieces.

2 To make the vinaigrette, put all the ingredients into a screw-top jar and shake vigorously to combine. Adjust the seasoning to taste if necesary.

3 Toast the French bread under the grill or in the oven until dry and golden brown, then lightly rub with the peeled garlic clove.

4 Trim the French beans, cut into 5 cm/2 in lengths and cook in boiling water until just tender. Drain and rinse under cold running water.

5 Wash the spinach, discarding the stalks, and tear into small pieces. Arrange on individual serving plates with the celery, French beans, sun-dried tomatoes, chicken and spring onions.

6 Spoon over the vinaigrette dressing. Arrange the toasted slices of French bread on top, garnish with fresh chives and parsley and serve immediately.

Warm Chicken Salad

Succulent chicken pieces are combined with vegetables and rice in a light chilli dressing.

INGREDIENTS

Serves 6

50 g/2 oz mixed salad leaves

50 g/2 oz baby spinach leaves

50 g/2 oz watercress

30 ml/2 tbsp chilli sauce

30 ml/2 tbsp dry sherry

15 ml/1 tbsp light soy sauce

15 ml/1 tbsp tomato ketchup

10 ml/2 tsp olive oil

8 shallots, finely chopped

1 garlic clove, crushed

350 g/12 oz skinless, boneless chicken
   breast, cut into thin strips

1 red pepper, seeded and sliced

175 g/6 oz mangetouts, trimmed

400 g/14 oz can baby corn cobs, drained
   and halved

275 g/10 oz brown rice, cooked

salt and ground black pepper

fresh parsley sprig, to garnish

1 If any of the mixed salad leaves are large, tear them into smaller pieces and arrange with the spinach leaves on a serving dish. Add the watercress and toss together to mix.

2 In a small bowl, mix together the chilli sauce, sherry, soy sauce and tomato ketchup. Set the sauce mixture aside.

3 Heat the oil in a large, non-stick frying pan or wok. Add the shallots and garlic and stir-fry over a medium heat for 1 minute.

4 Add the chicken to the pan and stir-fry for a further 3–4 minutes.

5 Add the pepper, mangetouts, baby corn cobs and rice, and stir-fry for a further 2–3 minutes.

6 Pour in the chilli sauce mixture and stir-fry for 2–3 minutes, until hot and bubbling. Season to taste.

7 Spoon the chicken mixture over the salad leaves, toss together to mix and serve immediately, garnished with a sprig of fresh parsley.

VARIATION

Use other lean meat such as turkey breast, beef or pork in place of the chicken.

Spicy Chicken Salad

Marinate the chicken in advance for this tasty salad, which is otherwise quick to prepare.

INGREDIENTS

Serves 6

5 ml/1 tsp ground cumin seeds
5 ml/1 tsp paprika
5 ml/1 tsp ground turmeric
1–2 garlic cloves, crushed
30 ml/2 tbsp lime juice
4 chicken breasts, skinned and boned
225 g/8 oz rigatoni
1 red pepper, seeded and chopped
2 celery sticks, thinly sliced
1 shallot or small onion, finely chopped
25 g/1 oz/¼ cup stuffed green olives, halved
30 ml/2 tbsp clear honey
15 ml/1 tbsp wholegrain mustard
15–30 ml/1–2 tbsp lime juice
mixed salad leaves
salt and ground black pepper

2 Preheat the oven to 200°C/400°F/Gas 6. Put the chicken on a grill rack in a single layer and bake for 20 minutes. (Alternatively grill for 8–10 minutes on each side.)

3 Cook the rigatoni pasta in a large pan of boiling, salted water until *al dente*. Drain and rinse under cold water. Leave to drain thoroughly.

4 Put the red pepper, celery, shallot or small onion and olives into a large bowl with the pasta. Mix together.

5 Mix the honey, mustard and lime juice together in a small bowl and pour over the pasta mixture. Toss to coat.

6 Cut the chicken breasts into bite-size pieces. Arrange the mixed salad leaves on a serving dish, spoon the pasta mixture into the centre and top with the spicy chicken pieces.

1 Mix the cumin, paprika, turmeric, garlic and lime juice in a bowl. Season with salt and pepper. Rub this mixture over the chicken breasts. Lay these in a shallow dish, cover with clear film and leave in a cool place for about 3 hours or overnight.

Chicken Maryland Salad

Grilled chicken, sweetcorn, bacon, banana and watercress combine in a sensational main-course salad. Serve with jacket potatoes topped with a knob of butter.

INGREDIENTS

Serves 4

4 boneless free-range chicken breasts

oil, for brushing

225 g/8 oz rindless unsmoked bacon

4 sweetcorn cobs

45 ml/3 tbsp soft butter (optional)

4 ripe bananas, peeled and halved

4 firm tomatoes, halved

1 escarole or butterhead lettuce

1 bunch watercress

salt and ground black pepper

For the dressing

75 ml/5 tbsp groundnut oil

15 ml/1 tbsp white wine vinegar

10 ml/2 tsp maple syrup

10 ml/2 tsp prepared mild mustard

1 Season the chicken breasts, brush with oil and barbecue or grill for 15 minutes, turning once. Barbecue or grill the bacon for 8–10 minutes, or until crisp.

2 Bring a large saucepan of salted water to the boil. Shuck and trim the corn cobs or leave the husks on if you prefer. Boil for 20 minutes.

3 For extra flavour, brush the corn cobs with butter and brown over the barbecue or under the grill. Barbecue or grill the bananas and tomatoes for 6–8 minutes; you can brush these with butter too if you wish.

4 To make the dressing, combine the oil, vinegar, maple syrup and mustard with 15 ml/1 tbsp water in a screw-top jar and shake well.

5 Wash the lettuce and watercress leaves and spin dry. Put into a large bowl, pour over the dressing and toss well.

6 Distribute the salad leaves between four large serving plates. Slice the chicken and arrange over the salad leaves together with the bacon, banana, sweetcorn and tomatoes.

Chicken, Tongue and Gruyère Cheese Salad

The rich, sweet flavours of this salad marry well with the tart, peppery watercress. A minted lemon dressing freshens the overall effect. Serve with warm new potatoes.

INGREDIENTS

Serves 4

2 free-range chicken breasts, skinned and boned

½ chicken stock cube

225 g/8 oz ox tongue or ham, sliced 5 mm/ ¼ in thick

225 g/8 oz Gruyère cheese

1 lollo rosso lettuce

1 butterhead or endive lettuce

1 bunch watercress

2 green-skinned apples, cored and sliced

3 celery sticks, sliced

60 ml/4 tbsp sesame seeds, toasted

salt, ground black pepper and freshly grated nutmeg

For the dressing

75 ml/5 tbsp groundnut or sunflower oil

5 ml/1 tsp sesame oil

45 ml /3 tbsp lemon juice

10 ml/2 tsp chopped fresh mint

3 drops Tabasco sauce

2 To make the dressing, measure the oils, lemon juice, mint and Tabasco sauce into a screw-top jar and shake well. Cut the chicken, tongue or ham and cheese into fine strips. Moisten with a little dressing and set aside.

3 Combine the lettuce and watercress leaves with the apple and celery. Add the dressing and toss. Distribute between four large serving plates. Pile the chicken, tongue or ham and cheese in the centre, scatter with sesame seeds, season with salt, pepper and freshly grated nutmeg and serve.

1 Place the chicken breasts in a shallow saucepan, cover with 300 ml/½ pint/1¼ cups water, add the ½ stock cube and bring to the boil. Put the lid on the pan and simmer for 15 minutes. Drain, reserving the stock for another occasion, then cool the chicken under cold running water.

Curried Chicken Salad

A smooth, mildly spicy sauce with the distinctive tang of fresh coriander leaves blends with lean chicken pieces on a bed of pasta and vegetables.

INGREDIENTS

Serves 4

2 cooked chicken breasts, skinned and boned

175 g/6 oz French beans

350 g/12 oz multi-coloured penne

150 ml/¼ pint/⅔ cup plain yogurt

5 ml/1 tsp mild curry powder

1 garlic clove, crushed

1 green chilli, seeded and finely chopped

30 ml/2 tbsp chopped fresh coriander

4 firm ripe tomatoes, skinned, seeded and cut in strips

salt and ground black pepper

fresh coriander leaves, to garnish

1 Cut the chicken into strips. Cut the French beans into 2.5 cm/ 1 in lengths and cook in boiling water for 5 minutes. Drain and rinse under cold water.

2 Cook the pasta in a large pan of boiling, salted water until *al dente*. Drain and rinse thoroughly.

3 To make the sauce, mix the yogurt, curry powder, garlic, chilli and chopped coriander together in a bowl. Stir in the chicken pieces and leave to stand for 30 minutes.

4 Transfer the pasta to a large serving bowl and toss with the beans and tomatoes. Spoon over the chicken and sauce mixture. Garnish with the coriander leaves and serve.

"Poor Boy" Steak Salad

"Poor Boy" started life in the Italian Creole community of New Orleans when the poor survived on sandwiches filled with left-over scraps. Times have improved since then, and today the "Poor Boy" sandwich is commonly filled with tender beef steak and other goodies. This is a salad version of "Poor Boy".

INGREDIENTS

Serves 4

4 sirloin or rump steaks, each about
   175 g/6 oz
1 escarole lettuce
1 bunch watercress
4 tomatoes, quartered
4 large gherkins, sliced
4 spring onions, sliced
4 canned artichoke hearts, halved
175 g/6 oz button mushrooms, sliced
12 green olives
120 ml/4 fl oz/½ cup French Dressing
salt and ground black pepper

1 Season the steaks with black pepper. Cook under a moderate grill for 6–8 minutes, turning once, until medium-rare. Cover and leave to rest in a warm place.

2 Combine the lettuce and watercress leaves with the tomatoes, gherkins, spring onions, artichoke hearts, mushrooms and olives and toss with the French Dressing.

3 Divide the salad between four serving plates. Slice each steak diagonally and arrange over the salad. Season with salt and serve immediately.

Waldorf Ham Salad

Waldorf Salad first appeared at the Waldorf-Astoria Hotel, New York, in the 1890s. Originally it consisted of apples, celery and mayonnaise, and was commonly served with duck, ham and goose. This modern-day version often includes meat and is something of a meal in itself.

INGREDIENTS

Serves 4

3 apples

15 ml/1 tbsp lemon juice

2 slices cooked ham, each about 175 g/6 oz

2 celery stalks

150 ml/¼ pint/⅔ cup mayonnaise

1 escarole or endive lettuce

1 small radicchio, finely shredded

½ bunch watercress

45 ml/3 tbsp walnut or olive oil

50 g/2 oz/½ cup broken walnuts, toasted

salt and ground black pepper

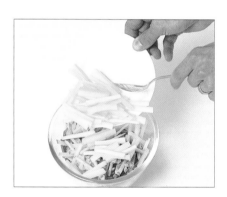

1 Peel, core, slice and finely shred the apples. Moisten with lemon juice to keep them white. Cut the ham into 5 cm/2 in strips. Cut the celery stalks into similar-sized pieces. Combine the apples, ham and celery in a bowl.

2 Add the mayonnaise and mix thoroughly.

3 Shred all the salad leaves finely, then moisten with oil. Distribute the leaves between four serving plates. Pile the mayonnaise mixture in the centre, scatter with toasted walnuts, season and serve.

Chicken Liver, Bacon and Tomato Salad

Warm salads are especially welcome during the autumn months when the days are growing shorter and cooler. This rich salad includes sweet spinach and the bitter leaves of frisée lettuce.

INGREDIENTS

Serves 4

225 g/8 oz young spinach, stems removed

1 frisée lettuce

105 ml/7 tbsp groundnut or sunflower oil

175 g/6 oz rindless unsmoked bacon, cut into strips

75 g/3 oz day-old bread, crusts removed and cut into short fingers

450 g/1lb chicken livers

115 g/4 oz cherry tomatoes

salt and ground black pepper

1 Place the spinach and lettuce leaves in a salad bowl. Heat 60 ml/4 tbsp of the oil in a large frying pan, add the bacon and cook for 3–4 minutes, or until crisp and brown. Remove the bacon with a slotted spoon and drain on kitchen paper.

2 To make croûtons, fry the bread in the bacon-flavoured oil, tossing until crisp and golden. Drain on kitchen paper.

3 Heat the remaining 45 ml/ 3 tbsp oil in the frying pan, add the chicken livers and fry briskly for 2–3 minutes. Turn the chicken livers out over the salad leaves and add the bacon, croûtons and tomatoes. Season, toss and serve warm.

VARIATION

If you can't find any baby spinach leaves you can use lamb's lettuce. Watercress would make a deliciously peppery substitute, but you should use less of it and bulk the salad out with a milder leaf so that the watercress doesn't overwhelm the other flavours.

Curry Fried Pork and Rice Vermicelli Salad

Pork crackling adds a delicious crunch to this popular salad.

INGREDIENTS

Serves 4

225 g/8 oz lean pork

2 garlic cloves, finely chopped

2 slices fresh root ginger, peeled and finely chopped

30–45 ml/2–3 tbsp rice wine

45 ml/3 tbsp vegetable oil

2 lemon grass stalks, finely chopped

10 ml/2 tsp curry powder

175 g/6 oz/³⁄₄ cup beansprouts

225 g/8 oz rice vermicelli, soaked in warm water until soft then drained

¹⁄₂ lettuce, finely shredded

30 ml/2 tbsp fresh mint leaves

lemon juice and Thai fish sauce, to taste

salt and ground black pepper

2 spring onions, chopped, 25 g/1 oz/ ¹⁄₄ cup toasted peanuts, chopped, and pork crackling (optional) to garnish

1 Cut the pork into thin strips. Place in a shallow dish with half the garlic and ginger. Season with salt and pepper, pour over 30 ml/2 tbsp rice wine and marinate for at least 1 hour.

2 Heat the oil in a frying pan. Add the remaining garlic and ginger and fry for a few seconds until fragrant and golden. Stir in the strips of pork, with the marinade, and add the lemon grass and curry powder.

3 Fry on a high heat until the pork is golden and cooked through, adding more rice wine if the mixture seems too dry.

4 Place the beansprouts in a sieve. Blanch them by lowering the sieve into a saucepan of boiling water for 1 minute, then drain and refresh under cold running water. Drain again. Using the same water, cook the rice vermicelli for 3–5 minutes, until tender. Drain and rinse under cold running water.

5 Drain the vermicelli well and tip into a large bowl. Add the beansprouts, shredded lettuce and mint leaves. Season with lemon juice and fish sauce to taste. Toss lightly to combine the flavours.

6 Divide the vermicelli mixture among individual serving plates, making a nest on each plate. Arrange the pork mixture on top. Garnish with spring onions, toasted peanuts and pork crackling, if using. Serve.

Sweet Potato, Egg, Pork and Beetroot Salad

This dish is a delicious way to use up left-over roast pork. Sweet flavours balance well with the bitterness of the chicory leaves.

INGREDIENTS

Serve 4

900 g/2 lb sweet potatoes

4 chicory heads

5 eggs, hard-boiled

450 g/1 lb pickled young beetroot

175 g/6 oz cold roast pork

salt

For the dressing

75 ml/5 tbsp groundnut or sunflower oil

30 ml/2 tbsp white wine vinegar

10 ml/2 tsp Dijon mustard

5 ml/1 tsp fennel seeds, crushed

1 Peel the sweet potatoes and dice into equal-sized pieces.

2 Add the diced sweet potatoes to a pan of boiling salted water. Bring back to the boil then simmer for 10–15 minutes, or until the potatoes are soft. Drain and allow to cool.

3 To make the dressing, combine the oil, vinegar, mustard and fennel seeds in a screw-top jar and shake.

4 Separate the chicory leaves and arrange them around the edge of four serving plates.

5 Pour two thirds of the dressing over the sweet potatoes, stir in so that all the pieces of potato are coated in the dressing, and spoon on top of the chicory leaves.

6 Shell the hard-boiled eggs. Slice the eggs and beetroot, and arrange to make an attractive circle around the sweet potato.

7 Slice the pork then cut into strips of around 4 cm/1½ in. Place in a bowl and moisten with the rest of the dressing.

8 Pile the strips of pork into the centre of each salad. Season with salt and serve.

COOK'S TIP

To crush the fennel seeds, grind using a pestle and mortar. If you don't have these use two dessertspoons instead. For extra flavour try toasting the fennel seeds before crushing.

Frankfurter Salad with Mustard Dressing

This is a last-minute salad, which you can throw together using mostly store-cupboard ingredients.

INGREDIENTS

Serves 4

675 g/1½ lb small new potatoes, scrubbed or scraped

2 eggs

350 g/12 oz frankfurters

1 butterhead or endive lettuce

225 g/8 oz young spinach leaves, stems removed

salt and ground black pepper

For the dressing

45 ml/3 tbsp safflower oil

30 ml/2 tbsp olive oil

15 ml/1 tbsp white wine vinegar

10 ml/2 tsp mustard

5 ml/1 tsp caraway seeds, crushed

1 Bring the potatoes to the boil in salted water and simmer for about 15 minutes, or until tender. Drain, cover and keep warm. Hard-boil the eggs for 12 minutes. Refresh in cold water, shell and cut into quarters.

2 Score the frankfurter skins cork-screw fashion with a small knife, then cover with boiling water and simmer for about 5 minutes to heat through. Drain well, cover and keep warm.

3 To make the dressing, place all the ingredients in a screw-top jar and shake.

4 Moisten the salad leaves with half of the dressing and distribute between four large serving plates.

5 Moisten the warm potatoes and frankfurters with the remainder of the dressing and scatter over the salad.

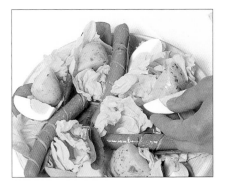

6 Finish the salad with sections of hard-boiled egg, season and serve warm.

COOK'S TIP

This salad has a German slant to it and calls for a sweet-and-sour German-style mustard. American mustards have a similar quality.

Smoked Bacon and Green Bean Pasta Salad

A tasty pasta salad, subtly flavoured with smoked bacon and tossed in a light, flavoursome dressing.

INGREDIENTS

Serves 4

350 g/12 oz wholewheat pasta twists

225 g/8 oz green beans

8 rashers lean smoked back bacon

350 g/12 oz cherry tomatoes, halved

2 bunches spring onions, chopped

400 g/14 oz can chick-peas, drained

For the dressing

90 ml/6 tbsp tomato juice

30 ml/2 tbsp balsamic vinegar

5 ml/1 tsp ground cumin

5 ml/1 tsp ground coriander

30 ml/2 tbsp chopped fresh coriander

salt and ground black pepper

2 Preheat the grill and cook the bacon for 2–3 minutes on each side, until cooked. Dice the bacon and add to the beans.

3 Put the tomatoes, spring onions and chick-peas in a large bowl. In a small bowl, mix together the tomato juice, vinegar, spices, fresh coriander and seasoning.

4 Pour the dressing into a large bowl. Drain the cooked pasta thoroughly and add to the tomato mixture with the green beans and bacon. Toss all the ingredients together to mix thoroughly. Serve warm or cold.

1 Cook the pasta in a large saucepan of lightly salted, boiling water until *al dente*. Meanwhile, trim and halve the green beans and cook them in boiling water for about 5 minutes, until tender. Drain thoroughly and keep warm.

COOK'S TIP

Always rinse canned beans and pulses well before using, to remove as much of the brine (salt water) as possible.

Warm Pasta Salad with Asparagus

This warm salad is served with ham, eggs and parmesan. A mustard dressing made from the thick part of the asparagus stalks provides a rich accompaniment.

INGREDIENTS

Serves 4

450 g/1 lb asparagus

450 g/1 lb dried tagliatelle

225 g/8 oz cooked ham, sliced 5 mm/¼in thick, and cut into fingers

2 eggs, hard-boiled and sliced

50 g/2 oz piece Parmesan cheese

For the dressing

50 g/2 oz cooked potato

75 ml/5 tbsp olive oil

15 ml/1 tbsp lemon juice

10 ml/2 tsp Dijon mustard

120 ml/4 fl oz/½ cup vegetable stock

salt and ground black pepper

1 Bring a saucepan of salted water to the boil. Trim and discard the tough, woody part of the asparagus stalks. Cut the asparagus in half and boil the thicker halves for 12 minutes, adding the asparagus tips after 6 minutes. Refresh under cold water until warm, then drain.

2 Finely chop 150 g/5 oz of the thicker asparagus pieces. Place in a food processor together with the dressing ingredients and process until smooth. Season the dressing to taste.

3 Boil the pasta in a large saucepan of salted water until *al dente*. Refresh under cold water.

4 Dress with the asparagus sauce and turn out into four pasta bowls. Top each pile of pasta with some of the ham, eggs and asparagus tips. Finish with shavings of Parmesan cheese and serve warm.

Devilled Ham and Pineapple Salad

This tasty salad, with a crunchy topping of toasted almonds, can be quickly prepared using items from the store-cupboard.

INGREDIENTS

Serves 4

225 g/8 oz wholewheat penne

150 ml/¼ pint/⅔ cup plain yogurt

15 ml/1 tbsp cider vinegar

5 ml/1 tsp wholegrain mustard

large pinch of caster sugar

30 ml/2 tbsp hot mango chutney

115 g/4 oz cooked lean ham, cubed

200 g/7 oz can pineapple chunks, drained

2 celery sticks, chopped

½ green pepper, seeded and diced

15 ml/1 tbsp toasted flaked almonds, chopped roughly

salt and ground black pepper

crusty bread, to serve

1 Cook the pasta in a large pan of salted boiling water until *al dente*. Drain and rinse thoroughly. Leave to cool.

2 To make the dressing, mix the yogurt, vinegar, mustard, sugar and mango chutney together. Season with salt and pepper. Add the pasta and toss lightly together.

3 Transfer the pasta to a serving dish. Add the ham, pineapple, celery and green pepper.

4 Sprinkle toasted almonds over the top of the salad. Serve with crusty bread.

Pear and Pecan Nut Salad

Toasted pecan nuts have a special affinity with crisp white pears. Their robust flavours combine well with a rich Blue Cheese and Chive dressing to make this a salad to remember.

INGREDIENTS

Serves 4

75 g/3 oz/½ cup shelled pecan nuts, roughly chopped

3 crisp pears

175 g/6 oz young spinach, stems removed

1 escarole or butterhead lettuce

1 radicchio

30 ml/2 tbsp Blue Cheese and Chive Dressing

salt and ground black pepper

crusty bread, to serve

1 Toast the pecan nuts under a moderate grill to bring out their flavour.

COOK'S TIP
The pecan nuts will burn very quickly under the grill, so keep constant watch over them and remove them as soon as they change colour.

2 Cut the pears into even slices, leaving the skins intact but discarding the cores.

3 Place the spinach, lettuce and radicchio leaves into a large bowl. Add the pears and toasted pecans, pour over the Blue Cheese and Chive Dressing and toss well. Distribute among four large serving plates and season with salt and pepper. Serve the salad with warm crusty bread.

Goat's Cheese and Fig Salad

Fresh figs and walnuts are perfect partners for goat's cheese and toasted buckwheat. The olive and nut oil dressing contains no vinegar, depending instead on the acidity of the goat's cheese.

INGREDIENTS

Serves 4

175 g/6 oz/1 cup couscous

30 ml/2 tbsp toasted buckwheat

1 egg, hard-boiled

30 ml/2 tbsp chopped fresh parsley

60 ml/4 tbsp olive oil

45 ml/3 tbsp walnut oil

115 g/4 oz rocket leaves

1/2 frisée lettuce

175 g/6 oz crumbly white goat's cheese

50 g/2 oz/1/2 cup broken walnuts, toasted

4 ripe figs, trimmed and almost cut into
    four (leave the pieces joined at the base)

1 Place the couscous and toasted buckwheat in a bowl, cover with boiling water and leave to soak for 15 minutes. Place in a sieve to drain off any remaining water, then spread out on a metal tray and allow to cool.

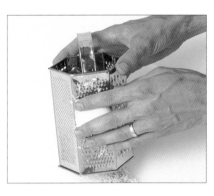

2 Shell the hard-boiled egg and grate finely.

3 Toss the grated egg, parsley, couscous and buckwheat together in a bowl. Combine the olive and walnut oils using half to moisten the couscous mixture.

4 Toss the salad leaves in the remaining oil and distribute between four large serving plates.

5 Pile the couscous mixture in the centre of each plate and crumble the goat's cheese over the top. Scatter with toasted walnuts, place a fig in the centre of each plate and serve.

COOK'S TIP

Goat's cheeses vary in strength from the youngest, which are soft and mild, to strongly-flavoured, mature cheeses, which have a firm and crumbly texture. The crumbly varieties are best suited to salads.

Avocado, Tomato and Mozzarella Salad

This popular salad is made from ingredients representing the colours of the Italian flag – a sunny, cheerful dish! The addition of pasta turns it into a main course meal for a light lunch.

INGREDIENTS

Serves 4

175 g/6 oz pasta bows (farfalle)

6 ripe red tomatoes

225 g/8 oz mozzarella cheese

1 large ripe avocado

30 ml/2 tbsp chopped fresh basil

30 ml/2 tbsp pine nuts, toasted

fresh basil sprig, to garnish

For the dressing

90 ml/6 tbsp olive oil

30 ml/2 tbsp wine vinegar

5 ml/1 tsp balsamic vinegar (optional)

5 ml/1 tsp wholegrain mustard

pinch of sugar

salt and ground black pepper

1 Cook the pasta bows in plenty of salted, boiling water until *al dente*.

2 Slice the tomatoes and mozzarella cheese into thin rounds.

3 Halve the avocado, remove the stone and peel off the skin. Slice the flesh lengthways.

4 Whisk the dressing ingredients together in a small bowl.

5 Arrange the tomato, mozzarella and avocado slices in overlapping slices around the edge of a flat serving plate.

6 Toss the pasta with half of the dressing and the chopped basil. Pile into the centre of the plate. Pour over the remaining dressing, scatter over the pine nuts and garnish with a sprig of fresh basil. Serve immediately.

COOK'S TIP

The pale green flesh of the avocado quickly discolours once it is cut. Prepare it at the last minute and place immediately in dressing. If you do have to prepare it ahead, squeeze lemon juice over the cut side and cover with clear film.

Roquefort and Walnut Pasta Salad

This is a simple, earthy salad, relying totally on the quality of the ingredients. There is no real substitute for the Roquefort – a blue-veined ewe's-milk cheese from south-western France.

INGREDIENTS

Serves 4

225 g/8 oz pasta shapes

selection of salad leaves such as rocket, curly endive, lamb's lettuce, baby spinach, radicchio

30 ml/2 tbsp walnut oil

60 ml/4 tbsp sunflower oil

30 ml/2 tbsp red wine vinegar or sherry vinegar

225 g/8 oz Roquefort cheese, roughly crumbled

115 g/4 oz/1 cup walnut halves

salt and ground black pepper

3 Pile the pasta in the centre of the salad leaves, scatter over the crumbled Roquefort and pour over the dressing.

4 Scatter the walnuts over the top. Toss the salad just before serving.

1 Cook the pasta in plenty of salted, boiling water until *al dente*. Drain well and cool. Place the salad leaves in a bowl.

2 Whisk together the walnut oil, sunflower oil and vinegar. Season with salt and pepper to taste.

COOK'S TIP

Toast the walnuts under the grill to add extra flavour.

Pasta, Asparagus and Potato Salad

Made with wholewheat pasta, this delicious salad is a real treat, especially when made with fresh asparagus just in season.

INGREDIENTS

Serves 4

225 g/8 oz wholewheat pasta shapes

60 ml/4 tbsp extra-virgin olive oil

350 g/12 oz baby new potatoes

225 g/8 oz asparagus

115 g/4 oz piece Parmesan cheese

salt and ground black pepper

1 Cook the pasta in salted, boiling water until *al dente*.

2 Drain well and toss with the olive oil while the pasta is still warm. Season with salt and ground black pepper.

3 Scrub the potatoes and cook in boiling salted water for about 15 minutes, or until tender. Drain the potatoes and toss together with the pasta.

4 Trim any woody ends off the asparagus and halve the stalks if very long. Blanch in boiling salted water for 6 minutes, until bright green and still crunchy. Drain. Plunge into cold water to stop the asparagus cooking and allow to cool. Drain and dry on kitchen paper.

5 Toss the asparagus with the potatoes and pasta, adjust the seasoning to taste and transfer to a shallow serving bowl. Using a vegetable peeler, shave the Parmesan over the salad.

Courgettes, Carrots and Pecan Salad

Chunks of warm fried courgettes are served with a crisp tangy salad in pockets of pitta bread.

INGREDIENTS

Serves 2

2 carrots
25 g/1 oz/¼ cup pecan nuts
4 spring onions, sliced
50 ml/2 fl oz/¼ cup Greek yogurt
35 ml/7 tsp olive oil
5 ml/1 tsp lemon juice
15 ml/1 tbsp chopped fresh mint
2 courgettes
25 g/1 oz/¼ cup plain flour
2 pitta breads
salt and ground black pepper
shredded lettuce, to serve

3 In a clean bowl, make the dressing. Whisk the yogurt with 7.5 ml/1½ tsp of the olive oil, the lemon juice and the mint. Stir the dressing into the carrot mixture and mix well. Cover and chill until required.

5 Heat the remaining oil in a large frying pan. Add the coated courgette slices and cook for 3–4 minutes, turning once, until browned. Drain the courgettes on kitchen paper.

1 Top and tail the carrots. Grate them coarsely into a bowl.

4 Top and tail the courgettes. Cut them diagonally into slices. Season the flour with salt and pepper. Spread it out on a plate and turn the courgette slices in it until they are well coated.

6 Make a slit in each pitta bread to form a pocket. Fill the pittas with the carrot mixture and the courgette slices. Serve on a bed of shredded lettuce.

2 Stir in the pecans and spring onions and toss well.

COOK'S TIP

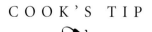

Warm the pitta breads in the oven or under a medium grill. Do not fill the pitta breads too soon or the carrot mixture will make the bread soggy.

Pasta, Olive and Avocado Salad

The ingredients of this salad are united by a wonderful sun-dried tomato and fresh basil dressing.

INGREDIENTS

Serves 6

225 g/8 oz pasta spirals or other small pasta shapes

115 g/4 oz can sweetcorn, drained, or frozen sweetcorn, thawed

1/2 red pepper, seeded and diced

8 black olives, pitted and sliced

3 spring onions, finely chopped

2 medium avocados

For the dressing

2 sun-dried tomato halves, loose-packed (not preserved in oil)

25 ml/1 1/2 tbsp balsamic or white wine vinegar

25 ml/1 1/2 tbsp red wine vinegar

1/2 garlic clove, crushed

2.5 ml/1/2 tsp salt

75 ml/5 tbsp olive oil

15 ml/1 tbsp chopped fresh basil

1 To make the dressing, drop the sun-dried tomatoes into a pan containing 2.5 cm/1 in boiling water and simmer for about 3 minutes until tender. Drain and chop finely.

2 Combine the sun-dried tomatoes, both vinegars, garlic and salt in a food processor. With the machine on, add the olive oil in a stream. Stir in the basil.

3 Cook the pasta in a large pan of salted boiling water until *al dente*. Drain well. In a large bowl, combine the pasta, sweetcorn, red pepper, olives and spring onions. Add the dressing and toss well.

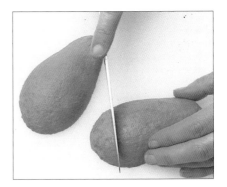

4 Just before serving, peel and stone the avocados and cut the flesh into cubes. Mix gently into the pasta then place the salad on a serving dish. Serve at room temperature.

Roast Pepper and Mushroom Pasta Salad

A combination of grilled peppers and two different kinds of mushroom makes this salad colourful as well as nutritious.

INGREDIENTS

Serves 6

1 red pepper, halved

1 yellow pepper, halved

1 green pepper, halved

350 g/12 oz wholewheat pasta shells
  or twists

30 ml/2 tbsp olive oil

45 ml/3 tbsp balsamic vinegar

75 ml/5 tbsp tomato juice

30 ml/2 tbsp chopped fresh basil

15 ml/1 tbsp chopped fresh thyme

175 g/6 oz/2¼ cups shiitake
  mushrooms, diced

175 g/6 oz/2¼ cups oyster
  mushrooms, sliced

400 g/14 oz can black-eyed beans, drained
  and rinsed

115 g/4 oz/¾ cup sultanas

2 bunches spring onions, finely chopped

salt and ground black pepper

1 Preheat the grill to hot. Put the peppers cut-side down on a grill pan rack and place under the grill for 10–15 minutes, until the skins are charred. Cover the peppers with a clean, damp tea towel and set aside to cool.

2 Meanwhile, cook the pasta shells or twists in lightly salted, boiling water until *al dente*, then drain thoroughly.

3 Mix together the oil, vinegar, tomato juice, basil and thyme, add to the warm pasta and toss.

4 Remove and discard the skins from the peppers. Seed and slice and add to the pasta.

5 Add the mushrooms, beans, sultanas, spring onions and seasoning. Toss the ingredients to mix and serve immediately. Alternatively, cover and chill in the fridge before serving.

Mediterranean Pasta Salad

A type of Salade Niçoise with pasta, conjuring up all the sunny flavours of the Mediterranean.

INGREDIENTS

Serves 4

225 g/8 oz chunky pasta shapes
175 g/6 oz fine green beans
2 large ripe tomatoes
50 g/2 oz fresh basil leaves
200 g/7 oz can tuna fish in oil, drained
2 hard-boiled eggs, shelled and sliced
    or quartered
50 g/2 oz can anchovy fillets, drained
capers and black olives, to taste

For the dressing
90 ml/6 tbsp extra-virgin olive oil
30 ml/2 tbsp white wine vinegar or
    lemon juice
2 garlic cloves, crushed
2.5 ml/½ tsp Dijon mustard
30 ml/2 tbsp chopped fresh basil
salt and ground black pepper

1 To make the dressing, whisk all the ingredients together in a small bowl. Leave to infuse while you prepare the salad.

COOK'S TIP

Don't be tempted to chill this salad – the flavour will be dulled.

2 Cook the pasta in plenty of salted, boiling water until *al dente*. Drain well and cool.

3 Top and tail the green beans and blanch in salted, boiling water for 3 minutes. Drain and refresh in cold water.

4 Slice the tomatoes and arrange on the bottom of a serving bowl. Moisten with a little dressing and cover with a quarter of the basil leaves. Then cover with the beans. Moisten with a little more dressing and cover with a third of the remaining basil.

5 Cover the vegetables with the pasta tossed in a little more dressing, half the remaining basil and the roughly flaked tuna.

6 Arrange the eggs on top, then finally scatter over the anchovy fillets, capers and olives. Spoon over the remaining dressing and garnish with the remaining basil. Serve immediately.

SPECIAL
OCCASION SALADS

Gado Gado

This classic Indonesian vegetable salad is served with a delicious hot peanut sauce.

INGREDIENTS

Serves 4–6

2 medium potatoes

175 g/6 oz French beans, topped and tailed

175 g/6 oz Chinese leaves, shredded

1 iceberg lettuce

175 g/6 oz beansprouts

½ cucumber, cut into fingers

150 g/5 oz daikon radish, shredded

3 spring onions

225 g/8 oz beancurd, cut into large slices

3 hard-boiled eggs, shelled and quartered

1 small bunch fresh coriander

prawn crackers, to serve

For the peanut sauce

150 g/5 oz/1¼ cups raw peanuts

15 ml/1 tbsp vegetable oil

2 shallots or 1 small onion, finely chopped

1 garlic clove, crushed

1–2 small chillies, seeded and finely chopped

1 cm/½ in square shrimp paste or 15 ml/ 1 tbsp Thai fish sauce (optional)

30 ml/2 tbsp tamarind sauce

120 ml/4 fl oz/½ cup canned coconut milk

15 ml/1 tbsp clear honey

1 Peel the potatoes. Bring to the boil in salted water and simmer for about 15 minutes, or until tender. Cook the French beans for 3–4 minutes. Drain the potatoes and beans and refresh under cold running water.

2 To make the peanut sauce, dry-fry the peanuts in a wok, or place under a moderate grill, tossing them all the time to prevent burning.

3 Turn the peanuts on to a clean cloth and rub them vigorously with your hands to remove the papery skins. Place the peanuts in a food processor and blend for 2 minutes until finely crushed.

4 Heat the vegetable oil in a wok and soften the shallots or onion, garlic and chillies without letting them colour. Add the shrimp paste or fish sauce, if using, together with the tamarind sauce, coconut milk and honey.

5 Simmer briefly, add to the blended peanuts and process to form a thick sauce. Transfer to a small serving bowl and keep hot.

6 Arrange the potatoes, French beans and all the other salad ingredients on a large serving platter. Serve with the bowl of peanut sauce and prawn crackers.

Composed Salads

Composed salads make perfect starters. They are light and colourful and lend themselves to endless variation – and the components can often be prepared ahead for quick assembly.

The French are masters of the composed salad. Any combination of ingredients can be used – let your imagination and your palate guide you. Arranged attractively on a plate or in a bowl, this type of salad offers contrasting flavours, textures and colours. Raw or cooked vegetables, fresh fruits, hard-boiled hen's or quail's eggs, smoked or cooked poultry, meat, fish or shellfish can all be used, but it is important that the dressing or other seasoning unites all the elements harmoniously.

Unlike a tossed salad such as Salade de Mesclun, in which the leaves are tossed together with a simple vinaigrette, the components of a composed salad are kept more separate. The ingredients might be arranged in groups, sometimes on a base of lettuce or other leaves, or simply arranged in circles on the plate. Composed salads, like the famous Salade Niçoise or any of the following salads, are often served as a first course or a light main course, especially in warm weather. A tossed green salad is frequently eaten after the main course and is generally thought to cleanse the palate in preparation for the cheese course or dessert.

PRAWN, AVOCADO AND CITRUS SALAD

INGREDIENTS

Serves 6

15 ml/1 tbsp lemon juice
15 ml/1 tbsp lime juice
15 ml/1 tbsp clear honey
45 ml/3 tbsp olive oil
30–45 ml/2–3 tbsp walnut oil
30 ml/2 tbsp snipped fresh chives
450 g/1 lb large cooked prawns, shelled and deveined
1 avocado, peeled, stoned and cut into small dice
1 pink grapefruit, peeled and segmented
1 large navel orange, peeled and segmented
30 ml/2 tbsp pine nuts, toasted (optional)
salt and ground black pepper

1 Blend the lemon and lime juices, salt and pepper and honey in a small bowl. Slowly whisk in the olive oil, then the walnut oil, to make a creamy dressing. Stir in the chives.

2 Arrange the prawns with the diced avocado and grapefruit and orange segments on individual serving plates. Drizzle over the dressing, sprinkle with the toasted pine nuts, if using, and serve.

SMOKED SALMON SALAD WITH DILL

INGREDIENTS

Serves 4

225 g/8 oz smoked salmon, thinly sliced
1 fennel bulb, thinly sliced
1 medium cucumber, seeded and cut into julienne strips
30 ml/2 tbsp lemon juice
120 ml/4 fl oz/½ cup extra-virgin olive oil
30 ml/2 tbsp chopped fresh dill, plus a few sprigs to garnish
ground black pepper
caviar, to garnish (optional)

1 Arrange the smoked salmon slices on four individual serving plates and arrange the slices of fennel alongside, together with the cucumber strips.

2 Mix together the lemon juice and pepper in a small bowl. Slowly whisk in the olive oil to make a creamy vinaigrette. Stir in the chopped dill.

3 Spoon a little vinaigrette over the fennel and cucumber. Drizzle the remaining vinaigrette over the smoked salmon and garnish with sprigs of dill. Top each salad with a spoonful of caviar, if you like, before serving.

CHICORY SALAD WITH ROQUEFORT

INGREDIENTS

Serves 4

30 ml/2 tbsp red wine vinegar
5 ml/1 tsp Dijon mustard
50 ml/2 oz/¼ cup walnut oil
15–30 ml/1–2 tbsp sunflower oil
2 white or red chicory heads
1 celery heart or 4 celery sticks, cut into julienne strips
75 g/3 oz/¾ cup walnut halves, lightly toasted
115 g/4 oz Roquefort cheese
salt and ground black pepper
fresh parsley sprigs, to garnish

1 Whisk together the vinegar, mustard and salt and pepper to taste in a small bowl. Slowly whisk in the oils, to make a vinaigrette.

2 Arrange the chicory on individual serving plates. Scatter over the celery and walnut halves. Crumble the Roquefort cheese on top of each salad, drizzle over a little vinaigrette and serve garnished with parsley sprigs.

Clockwise from far right: Prawn, Avocado and Citrus Salad; Smoked Salmon Salad with Dill; and Chicory Salad with Roquefort.

Thai Scented Fish Salad

For a tropical taste of the Far East, try this delicious fish salad scented with coconut, exotic fruits and warm Thai spices.

INGREDIENTS

Serves 4

350 g/12 oz fillet of red mullet, sea bream
    or snapper
1 cos lettuce
½ lollo biondo lettuce
1 pawpaw or mango, peeled and sliced
1 pithaya, peeled and sliced
1 large ripe tomato, cut into wedges
½ cucumber, peeled and cut into strips
3 spring onions, sliced

For the marinade

5 ml/1 tsp coriander seeds
5 ml/1 tsp fennel seeds
2.5 ml/½ tsp cumin seeds
5 ml/1 tsp caster sugar
2.5 ml/½ tsp hot chilli sauce
30 ml/2 tbsp garlic oil
salt

For the dressing

15 ml/1 tbsp creamed coconut
60 ml/4 tbsp groundnut or safflower oil
finely grated rind and juice of 1 lime
1 red chilli, seeded and finely chopped
5 ml/1 tsp sugar
45 ml/3 tbsp chopped fresh coriander
salt

1 Cut the fish into even strips and place them on a plate or in a shallow bowl.

2 To make the marinade, crush the coriander, fennel and cumin seeds together with the sugar. Add the chilli sauce, garlic oil and salt and combine.

3 Spread the marinade over the fish, cover and leave to stand in a cool place for at least 20 minutes – longer if you have time.

4 To make the dressing, place the creamed coconut and salt in a screw-top jar with 45 ml/ 3 tbsp boiling water and allow to dissolve. Add the oil, lime rind and juice, chilli, sugar and chopped coriander. Shake well and set aside.

5 Combine the lettuce leaves with the pawpaw or mango, pithaya, tomato, cucumber and spring onions. Toss with the dressing, then distribute between four large serving plates.

6 Heat a large non-stick frying-pan, add the fish and cook for 5 minutes, turning once. Place the cooked fish over the salad and serve at once.

COOK'S TIP

If planning ahead, you can leave the fish in the marinade for up to 8 hours. The dressing can also be made in advance, minus the fresh coriander. Store at room temperature and add the coriander when you are ready to assemble the salad.

San Francisco Salad

California is a salad-maker's paradise and is renowned for the healthiness of its produce. San Francisco has become the salad capital of California, although this recipe is in fact based on a salad served at the Chez Panisse restaurant in Berkeley.

INGREDIENTS

Serves 4

900 g/2 lb langoustines or Dublin
   Bay prawns
50 g/2 oz bulb fennel, sliced
2 ripe medium tomatoes, quartered, and
   4 small tomatoes
30 ml/2 tbsp olive oil, plus extra for
   moistening the salad leaves
60 ml/4 tbsp brandy
150 ml/¼ pint/⅔ cup dry white wine
200 ml/7 fl oz can lobster or crab bisque
30 ml/2 tbsp chopped fresh tarragon
45 ml/3 tbsp double cream
225 g/8 oz green beans, topped and tailed
2 oranges
175 g/6 oz lamb's lettuce
115 g/4 oz rocket leaves
½ frisée lettuce
salt and cayenne pepper

1 Bring a large saucepan of salted water to the boil, add the langoustines or Dublin Bay prawns and simmer for 10 minutes. Refresh under cold running water.

2 Pre-heat the oven to 220°C/ 425°F/Gas 7. Twist the tails from all but four of the langoustines or prawns – reserve these to garnish the dish. Peel the outer shell from the tail meat. Put the tail peelings, carapace and claws in a heavy roasting tray with the fennel and medium tomatoes. Toss with the olive oil and roast near the top of the oven for 20 minutes to bring out the flavours.

3 Remove the roasting tray from the oven and place it over a moderate heat on top of the stove. Add the brandy and ignite to release the flavour of the alcohol. Add the wine and simmer briefly.

4 Transfer the contents of the roasting tray to a food processor and reduce to a coarse purée: this will take only 10–15 seconds. Rub the purée through a fine nylon sieve into a bowl. Add the lobster or crab bisque, tarragon and cream. Season to taste with salt and a little cayenne pepper.

5 Bring a saucepan of salted water to the boil and cook the beans for 6 minutes. Drain and cool under running water. To segment the oranges, cut the peel from the top and bottom, and then from the sides, with a serrated knife. Loosen the segments by cutting between the membranes and the flesh with a small knife.

6 Moisten the salad leaves with olive oil and distribute between four serving plates. Fold the langoustine tails into the dressing and distribute between the plates. Add the beans, orange segments and small tomatoes. Garnish each plate with a whole langoustine and serve warm.

Millionaire's Lobster Salad

When money is no object and you're in a decadent mood, this salad will satisfy your every whim.

INGREDIENTS

Serves 4

1 medium lobster, live or cooked

1 bay leaf

1 fresh thyme sprig

675 g/1½ lb new potatoes, scrubbed

2 ripe tomatoes

4 oranges

½ frisée lettuce

175 g/6 oz lamb's lettuce leaves

60 ml/4 tbsp extra-virgin olive oil

200 g/7 oz can young artichokes in brine, quartered

1 small bunch fresh tarragon, chervil or flat-leaf parsley

salt

For the dressing

30 ml/2 tbsp frozen concentrated orange juice, thawed

75 g/3 oz/6 tbsp unsalted butter, diced

salt and cayenne pepper

1 If the lobster needs cooking, add to a large pan of boiling salted water with the bay leaf and thyme. Bring back to the boil and simmer for 15 minutes. Cool under running water.

2 Twist off the legs and claws, and separate the tail from the body. Break the claws with a hammer and remove the meat. Cut the tail piece open from the underside, slice the meat and set aside.

3 Bring the potatoes to the boil in salted water and simmer for about 15 minutes, until tender. Drain, cover and keep warm.

4 Cut a cross in the skin of the tomatoes, cover with boiling water and leave for 30 seconds. Cool under running water and slip off the skins. Halve the tomatoes, discard the seeds, then cut the flesh into large dice.

5 To segment the oranges, remove the peel from the top, bottom and sides with a serrated knife. With a small paring knife, loosen the orange segments by cutting between the flesh and the membranes, holding the fruit over a small bowl.

6 To make the dressing, measure the orange juice into a heatproof bowl and set it over a saucepan containing 2.5 cm/1 in simmering water. Heat the juice for 1 minute, turn off the heat, then whisk in the butter a little at a time until the dressing reaches a coating consistency.

7 Season to taste with salt and a pinch of cayenne pepper, cover and keep warm.

8 Dress the salad leaves with olive oil, then divide between four large serving plates. Moisten the potatoes, artichokes and orange segments with olive oil and distribute among the leaves.

9 Lay the sliced lobster over the salad, spoon on the warm dressing, add the diced tomato and decorate with the fresh herbs. Serve at room temperature.

Genoese Squid Salad

This is a good salad for summer, when French beans and new potatoes are at their best. Serve it for a first course or light lunch.

INGREDIENTS

Serves 4–6

450 g/1 lb prepared squid, cut into rings

4 garlic cloves, roughly chopped

300 ml/½ pint/1¼ cups Italian red wine

450 g/1 lb waxy new potatoes, scrubbed

225 g/8 oz French beans, trimmed and cut into short lengths

2–3 sun-dried tomatoes in oil, drained and thinly sliced lengthways

60 ml/4 tbsp extra-virgin olive oil

15 ml/1 tbsp red wine vinegar

salt and ground black pepper

1 Preheat the oven to 180°C/ 350°F/Gas 4. Put the squid rings in an earthenware dish with half the garlic, the wine and pepper to taste. Cover and cook for 45 minutes, or until the squid is tender.

2 Put the potatoes in a saucepan, cover with cold water and add a good pinch of salt. Bring to the boil, cover and simmer for about 15 minutes, until tender. Using a slotted spoon, lift out the potatoes and set aside. Add the beans to the boiling water and cook for 3 minutes. Drain.

3 When the potatoes are cool enough to handle, slice them thickly on the diagonal and place them in a bowl with the warm beans and sun-dried tomatoes. Whisk the oil, vinegar and the remaining garlic in a jug and add salt and pepper to taste. Pour over the potato mixture.

4 Drain the squid and discard the liquid. Add the squid to the potato mixture and mix very gently. Arrange on individual plates and season liberally with pepper.

COOK'S TIP

The French potato called Charlotte is perfect for this salad because it retains its shape when boiled. Prepared squid can be bought from supermarkets with fresh fish counters, and from fishmongers.

Tuna Carpaccio

Fillet of beef is most often used for carpaccio, but meaty fish like tuna – and swordfish – make an unusual change. The secret is to slice the fish wafer-thin, made possible by freezing it first, a technique used by the Japanese for making sashimi.

INGREDIENTS

Serves 4

2 fresh tuna steaks, about 450 g/1 lb total
    weight
60 ml/4 tbsp extra-virgin olive oil
15 ml/1 tbsp balsamic vinegar
5 ml/1 tsp caster sugar
30 ml/2 tbsp bottled green peppercorns
    or capers, drained
salt and ground black pepper
lemon wedges and green salad, to serve

1 Remove the skin from each tuna steak and place each steak between two sheets of clear film or non-stick baking paper. Pound with a rolling pin until the steak is flattened slightly.

2 Roll up the tuna steaks as tightly as possible, then wrap tightly in clear film. Place the tuna steaks in the freezer for 4 hours, or until firm.

3 Unwrap the tuna and cut crossways into the thinnest possible slices. Arrange the slices on individual serving plates.

4 Whisk together the oil, vinegar, sugar and peppercorns or capers, season and pour over the tuna. Cover and allow to come to room temperature for 30 minutes before serving with lemon wedges and green salad.

COOK'S TIP

Raw fish is safe to eat as long as it is very fresh, so check with your fishmonger before purchase and make and serve the carpaccio the same day. Do not buy fish that has been frozen and thawed.

Salade Mouclade

Mouclade is a long-established dish from La Rochelle in south-west France. The dish consists of mussels in a light curry cream sauce, and is usually served hot. Here the flavours appear in a salad of warm lentils and lightly cooked spinach. Serve at room temperature during the summer months.

INGREDIENTS

Serves 4

45 ml/3 tbsp olive oil

1 medium onion, finely chopped

350 g/12 oz/1½ cups puy or green lentils, soaked for 2 hours and drained

900 ml/1½ pints/3¾ cups vegetable stock

2 kg/4½ lb fresh mussels in their shells

75 ml/5 tbsp white wine

2.5 ml/½ tsp curry paste

pinch of saffron

30 ml/2 tbsp double cream

2 large carrots, peeled

4 celery sticks

900 g/2 lb young spinach, stems removed

15 ml/1 tbsp garlic oil

salt and cayenne pepper

1 Heat the oil in a heavy saucepan and soften the onion for 6–8 minutes. Add the lentils and vegetable stock, bring to the boil and simmer for 45 minutes. Remove from the heat and cool.

2 Clean the mussels thoroughly, discarding any that are damaged. Any that are open should close if given a sharp tap; if they fail to do so, discard these too.

3 Place the mussels in a large saucepan, add the wine, cover and steam over a high heat for 12 minutes. Strain the mussels in a colander, collecting the cooking liquor in a bowl, and discard any that have not opened during the cooking. Take all but four of the mussels out of their shells.

4 Pass the mussel liquor through a fine sieve or muslin into a wide, shallow pan to remove any grit or sand.

5 Add the curry paste and saffron, then reduce over a high heat until almost dry. Remove from the heat, stir in the cream, season and combine with the mussels.

6 Cut the carrot and celery into 5 cm/2 in matchsticks and cook in salted boiling water for 3 minutes. Drain, cool and moisten with olive oil.

7 Wash the spinach, put the wet leaves into a large saucepan, cover and steam for 30 seconds. Immerse in cold water then press the leaves dry in a colander. Moisten with garlic oil and season.

8 Spoon the lentils into the centre of four plates. Place heaps of spinach around the edge, with some carrot and celery on top. Spoon over the mussels and garnish with the reserved mussels in their shells.

Hot Coconut, Prawn and Pawpaw Salad

Transport yourself to the Far East with this wonderful dish that combines juicy pawpaw and succulent prawn tails in a spicy coconut dressing.

INGREDIENTS

Serves 4–6

225 g/8 oz raw or cooked prawn tails, peeled and deveined

2 ripe pawpaws

225 g/8 oz cos or iceberg lettuce leaves, Chinese leaves and young spinach leaves

1 firm tomato, peeled, seeded and roughly chopped

3 spring onions, shredded

1 small bunch fresh coriander, shredded, and 1 large chilli, sliced, to garnish

For the dressing

15 ml/1 tbsp creamed coconut

90 ml/6 tbsp vegetable oil

juice of 1 lime

2.5 ml/½ tsp hot chilli sauce

10 ml/2 tsp Thai fish sauce (optional)

5 ml/1 tsp sugar

2 If using raw prawn tails, cover with cold water in a saucepan, bring to the boil and simmer for no longer than 2 minutes. Drain and set aside.

3 Cut the pawpaws in half from top to bottom and remove the black seeds. Peel away the skin and cut the flesh into equal-size pieces.

4 Place the salad leaves in a bowl. Add the prawn tails, pawpaws, tomato and spring onions. Pour over the dressing, garnish with the coriander and chilli, and serve.

1 To make the dressing, place the creamed coconut in a screw-top jar and add 30 ml/2 tbsp boiling water to soften it. Add the oil, lime juice, chilli sauce, fish sauce, if using, and sugar. Shake well and set aside. Do not chill.

Roasted Chicken and Walnut Salad

The chickens may be cooked the day before eating and the salad finished on the day itself. Serve with warm garlic bread.

INGREDIENTS

Serves 8

4 fresh tarragon or rosemary sprigs

2 x 1.75 kg/4–4½ lb chickens

65 g/2½ oz/5 tbsp softened butter

150 ml/¼ pint/⅔ cup chicken stock

150 ml/¼ pint/⅔ cup white wine

115 g/4 oz/1 cup walnut pieces

1 small cantaloupe melon

lettuce leaves

450 g/1 lb seedless grapes or stoned cherries

salt and ground black pepper

For the dressing

30 ml/2 tbsp tarragon vinegar

120 ml/4 fl oz/½ cup light olive oil

30 ml/2 tbsp chopped fresh mixed herbs such as parsley, mint, tarragon

1 Preheat the oven to 200°C/400°F/Gas 6. Put the sprigs of tarragon or rosemary inside the chickens and season with salt and pepper.

2 Spread the chickens with 50 g/2 oz/4 tbsp of the softened butter, place in a roasting tin and pour the stock around. Cover loosely with foil and roast for about 1½ hours, basting twice, until browned and the juices run clear. Remove from the roasting tin and leave to cool.

3 Add the wine to the roasting tin. Bring to the boil on the stove and cook until syrupy. Strain and leave to cool. Heat the remaining butter in a frying pan and gently fry the walnuts until lightly browned. Scoop the melon flesh into balls or cut into cubes. Joint the chickens.

4 To make the dressing, whisk the vinegar and olive oil together with a little salt and pepper. Remove the fat from the chicken juices and add the juices to the dressing with the herbs. Adjust the seasoning to taste.

5 Arrange the chicken pieces on a bed of lettuce leaves, scatter over the grapes or cherries and melon, and spoon over the dressing. Sprinkle with the toasted walnuts and serve.

Chicken Liver Salad

This delicious salad may be served as a main course for a summer lunch party, or as a tasty first course served on individual plates. The richness of the chicken livers is complemented perfectly by the sweet tangy wholegrain mustard dressing. Serve with warm crusty bread to mop up the dressing.

INGREDIENTS

Serves 4

mixed salad leaves such as frisée, oakleaf
    lettuce, radicchio
1 avocado, diced
30 ml/2 tbsp lemon juice
2 pink grapefruit
350 g/12 oz chicken livers
30 ml/2 tbsp olive oil
1 garlic clove, crushed
salt and ground black pepper
whole fresh chives, to garnish

For the dressing
30 ml/2 tbsp lemon juice
60 ml/4 tbsp olive oil
2.5 ml/½ tsp wholegrain mustard
2.5 ml/½ tsp clear honey
15 ml/1 tbsp snipped fresh chives
salt and ground black pepper

1 To make the dressing, put the lemon juice, olive oil, mustard, honey and fresh chives into a screw-top jar, and shake vigorously. Season to taste with salt and freshly ground black pepper.

2 Arrange the previously washed and well drained mixed salad leaves attractively on a large serving plate.

3 Peel and dice the avocado and mix with the lemon juice to prevent browning. Add to the plate of mixed leaves.

4 Peel the grapefruit, removing as much of the white pith as possible. Split into segments and arrange with the leaves and avocado on the serving plate.

5 Dry the chicken livers on kitchen paper and remove any unwanted pieces.

6 Using a sharp knife, cut the larger chicken livers in half. Leave the smaller ones whole.

7 Heat the oil in a large frying pan. Stir-fry the chicken livers and garlic briskly until the livers are brown all over (they should be slightly pink inside).

8 Season the chicken livers to taste with salt and black pepper, remove from the pan and drain on kitchen paper.

9 Place the chicken livers, while still warm, onto the salad leaves and spoon over the dressing. Garnish with the whole chives and serve immediately.

Grilled Chicken Salad with Lavender

Lavender may seem an odd salad ingredient, but its delightful scent has a natural affinity with garlic, orange and other herbs. A serving of polenta makes this salad both filling and delicious.

INGREDIENTS

Serves 4

4 boneless chicken breasts

900 ml/1½ pints/3¾ cups light chicken
    stock

175 g/6 oz/1 cup fine polenta or corn meal

50 g/2 oz/4 tbsp butter

450 g/1 lb young spinach leaves

175 g/6 oz lamb's lettuce leaves

8 small tomatoes, halved

salt and ground black pepper

8 fresh lavender sprigs, to garnish

For the lavender marinade

6 fresh lavender flowers

10 ml/2 tsp finely grated orange rind

2 garlic cloves, crushed

10 ml/2 tsp clear honey

30 ml/2 tbsp olive oil

10 ml/2 tsp chopped fresh thyme

10 ml/2 tsp chopped fresh marjoram

salt

1 To make the marinade, strip the lavender flowers from their stems and combine with the orange rind, garlic, honey and a pinch of salt. Add the olive oil, thyme and marjoram. Slash the chicken deeply, spread over the mixture and leave to marinate in a cool place for at least 20 minutes.

2 To make the polenta, bring the chicken stock to the boil in a heavy saucepan. Add the fine polenta or corn meal in a steady stream, stirring all the time until thick: this will take 2–3 minutes. Turn the cooked polenta out on to a 2.5 cm/1 in deep buttered tray and allow to cool.

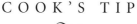

3 Heat the grill to a moderate temperature. (If using a barbecue, let the embers settle to a steady glow.) Grill the chicken breasts for about 15 minutes, turning them once.

COOK'S TIP

This lavender marinade is a delicious flavouring for salt-water fish as well as chicken. Try it spread over grilled cod, haddock, halibut, sea bass or bream.

4 Cut the cooled polenta into 2.5 cm/1 in cubes with a wet knife. Heat the remaining butter in a large frying-pan and fry the polenta cubes until golden brown.

5 Divide the salad leaves and tomatoes between four large serving plates. Slice each chicken breast and lay over the salad. Place the polenta cubes among the salad and season to taste. Garnish with the sprigs of lavender and serve.

Dijon Chicken Salad

This attractive and classical dish is ideal to serve for a simple but tasty and elegant lunch. Serve with extra salad leaves and some warm herb and garlic bread.

INGREDIENTS

Serves 4

4 skinless, boneless chicken breasts
mixed salad leaves such as frisée, oakleaf
    lettuce, radicchio

For the marinade
30 ml/2 tbsp tarragon wine vinegar
5 ml/1 tsp Dijon mustard
5 ml/1 tsp clear honey
90 ml/6 tbsp olive oil
salt and ground black pepper

For the mustard dressing
30 ml/2 tbsp Dijon mustard
3 garlic cloves, crushed
15 ml/1 tbsp grated onion
60 ml/4 tbsp white wine

1 To make the marinade mix the vinegar, mustard, honey, olive oil, salt and pepper together in a shallow glass or earthenware dish that is large enough to hold the chicken breasts in a single layer.

2 Add the chicken breasts to the dish, making sure they do not overlap each other.

3 Turn the chicken over in the marinade to coat completely, cover with clear film and chill in the fridge overnight.

4 Preheat the oven to 190°C/ 375°F/Gas 5. Transfer the chicken and the marinade into an ovenproof dish, cover with kitchen foil and bake for about 35 minutes, or until tender. Leave the chicken to cool in the liquid.

5 To make the mustard dressing, put all the ingredients into a screw-top jar and shake vigorously.

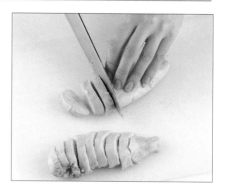

6 Thinly slice the chicken, and fan out the slices.

7 Arrange the chicken slices on a serving dish with the salad leaves. Spoon over some of the mustard dressing and serve. Serve the rest of the dressing separately in a bowl or jug.

COOK'S TIP

The dressing can be made several days in advance and stored in the fridge.

Duck Breast and Pasta Salad

The acidity of fruit is a very good accompaniment to a rich meat like duck as it adds a tartness which makes the meat more digestible. This luxurious salad includes apple, orange and, in the dressing, dried cherries. The pasta adds a welcome element of carbohydrate and makes the dish a complete meal.

INGREDIENTS

Serves 6

2 boneless duck breasts

salt and ground black pepper

5 ml/1 tsp coriander seeds, crushed

350 g/12 oz rigatoni

1 eating apple, diced

2 oranges, segmented

extra fresh chopped coriander and mint, to garnish

For the dressing

150 ml/¼ pint/⅔ cup orange juice

15 ml/1 tbsp lemon juice

10 ml/2 tsp clear honey

1 shallot, finely chopped

1 garlic clove, crushed

1 celery stick, chopped

75 g/3 oz dried cherries

45 ml/3 tbsp port

15 ml/1 tbsp chopped fresh mint

30 ml/2 tbsp chopped fresh coriander

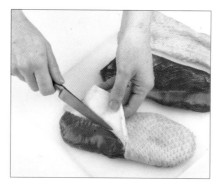

1 Preheat the grill. Remove the skin and fat from the duck breasts, season with salt and pepper and rub with the crushed coriander seeds.

2 Grill the duck breasts for 7–10 minutes (depending on the size). Wrap the duck breasts in foil and leave for 20 minutes.

3 Cook the pasta in a large pan of salted, boiling water, until *al dente*. Drain thoroughly and rinse under cold running water. Leave the pasta to cool.

4 To make the dressing, put the orange juice, lemon juice, honey, shallot, garlic, celery, cherries, port, mint and fresh coriander into a small bowl. Whisk together and leave to marinate for 30 minutes.

5 Unwrap the breasts from the foil and, using a very sharp carving knife, slice the duck very thinly. (It should still be slightly pink in the centre.)

6 Put the pasta into a large mixing bowl, add the dressing, diced apple and segments of orange. Toss well to coat the pasta.

7 Transfer the salad to a serving plate with the duck slices and garnish with the extra coriander and mint.

Duck Salad with Orange Sauce

The rich, gamey flavour of duck provides the foundation for this delicious salad. Serve it in late summer or autumn and enjoy the warm flavours of orange and coriander. Garlic croûtons add extra crunchy texture.

INGREDIENTS

Serves 4

1 small orange

2 boneless duck breasts

150 ml/¼ pint/⅔ cup dry white wine

5 ml/1 tsp ground coriander seeds

2.5 ml/½ tsp ground cumin or fennel seeds

30 ml/2 tbsp caster sugar

juice of ½ small lime or lemon

75 g/3 oz day-old bread, thickly sliced

45 ml/3 tbsp garlic oil

½ escarole lettuce

½ frisée lettuce

30 ml/2 tbsp sunflower or groundnut oil

salt and cayenne pepper

4 sprigs fresh coriander, to garnish

1 Halve the orange and slice thickly. Discard any pips and place the slices in a small saucepan. Cover with water, bring to the boil and simmer for 5 minutes to remove the bitterness. Drain the orange slices and set aside.

2 Pierce the skin of the duck breasts diagonally with a small knife (this will help release the fat). Rub the skin with salt.

3 Place a steel or cast-iron frying pan over a steady heat and cook the breasts for 20 minutes, turning once, until they are medium-rare. Transfer to a warm plate, cover and keep warm.

4 Heat the sediment in the frying pan until it begins to darken and caramelize. Add the wine and stir to loosen the sediment. Add the ground coriander, cumin or fennel seeds, sugar and orange slices.

5 Boil quickly and reduce to a coating consistency. Sharpen with the lime or lemon juice and season to taste with salt and cayenne pepper. Transfer the orange sauce to a bowl, cover and keep warm.

6 Remove the crusts from the bread and cut the bread into short fingers. Heat the garlic oil in a heavy frying pan and brown the croûtons. Season with salt, then turn out on to kitchen paper.

7 Moisten the salad leaves with a little sunflower or groundnut oil and distribute between four large serving plates.

8 Slice the duck breasts diagonally with a carving knife. Divide the meat into four and lift on to each salad plate. Spoon on the orange sauce, scatter with croûtons, decorate with a sprig of fresh coriander and serve warm.

Sesame Duck and Noodle Salad

This salad is complete in itself and makes a lovely summer lunch. The marinade is a marvellous blend of oriental flavours.

INGREDIENTS

Serves 4

2 boneless duck breasts

15 ml/1 tbsp oil

150 g/5 oz sugar snap peas

2 carrots, cut into 7.5 cm/3 in sticks

225 g/8 oz medium egg noodles

6 spring onions, sliced

salt

30 ml/2 tbsp fresh coriander leaves,
   to garnish

For the marinade

15 ml/1 tbsp sesame oil

5 ml/1 tsp ground coriander

5 ml/1 tsp five-spice powder

For the dressing

15 ml/1 tbsp vinegar

5 ml/1 tsp soft light brown sugar

5 ml/1 tsp soy sauce

1 garlic clove, crushed

15 ml/1 tbsp sesame seeds, toasted

45 ml/3 tbsp sunflower oil

30 ml/2 tbsp sesame oil

ground black pepper

1 Slice the duck breasts thinly across and place in a shallow dish. Mix together the ingredients for the marinade, pour over the duck and turn well to coat thoroughly. Cover and leave in a cool place for 30 minutes.

2 Heat the oil in a frying pan, add the slices of duck breast and stir-fry for 3–4 minutes, until cooked. Set aside.

3 Bring a saucepan of lightly salted water to the boil. Place the sugar snap peas and carrots in a steamer that will fit on top of the pan. When the water boils, add the noodles. Place the steamer on top and steam the vegetables while cooking the noodles.

4 Set the steamed vegetables aside. Drain the noodles, refresh under cold running water and drain again. Place them in a large serving bowl.

5 To make the dressing, mix the vinegar, sugar, soy sauce, garlic and sesame seeds in a bowl. Add a generous grinding of pepper, then whisk in the oils.

6 Pour the dressing over the noodles and mix well. Add the peas, carrots, spring onions and duck slices and toss to mix. Scatter the coriander leaves over the top and serve immediately.

Prosciutto Salad with an Avocado Fan

*Avocados are amazingly versatile –
they can serve as edible containers,
be sliced or diced in a salad, or form
the foundation of a delicious soup or
sauce. However, they are at their
most elegant when sliced thinly and
fanned on a plate.*

INGREDIENTS

Serves 4

3 avocados

150 g/5 oz prosciutto

75–115 g/3–4 oz rocket leaves

24 marinated black olives, drained

For the dressing

15 ml/1 tbsp balsamic vinegar

5 ml/1 tsp lemon juice

5 ml/1 tsp prepared English mustard

5 ml/1 tsp sugar

75 ml/5 tbsp olive oil

salt and ground black pepper

1 To make the dressing,
combine the balsamic vinegar,
lemon juice, mustard and sugar in
a bowl. Whisk in the oil, season to
taste and set aside.

2 Cut two of the avocados in
half. Remove the stones and
skins, and cut the flesh into 1 cm/
½ in thick slices. Toss with half the
dressing. Place the prosciutto,
avocado slices and rocket on four
serving plates. Sprinkle the olives
and the remaining dressing over
the top.

3 Halve, stone and peel the
remaining avocado. Slice each
half lengthways into eighths.
Gently draw a cannelle knife across
the quarters at 1 cm/½ in intervals
to create regular stripes.

4 Make four cuts lengthways
down each avocado eighth,
leaving 1 cm/½ in intact at the
end. Carefully fan out the slices
and arrange on the side of
each plate.

Melon and Parma Ham Salad

Sections of cool, fragrant melon covered with slices of air-dried ham make this a delicious starter. When fresh strawberries are in season, serve it with a savoury-sweet strawberry salsa.

INGREDIENTS

Serves 4

1 large melon (cantaloupe, Galia or
  Charentais)
175 g/6 oz Parma ham, thinly sliced

For the salsa
225 g/8 oz strawberries
5 ml/1 tsp caster sugar
30 ml/2 tbsp groundnut or sunflower oil
15 ml/1 tbsp orange juice
2.5 ml/½ tsp finely grated orange rind
2.5 ml/½ tsp grated fresh root ginger
salt and ground black pepper

1 Halve the melon and take the seeds out with a spoon. Cut the rind away with a paring knife, then slice the melon flesh thickly. Chill until ready to serve.

2 To make the salsa, hull the strawberries and cut them into large dice. Place in a small mixing bowl with the sugar and crush lightly to release the juices. Add the oil, orange juice and rind and ginger. Season with salt and a generous twist of black pepper.

3 Arrange the melon slices on a serving plate and lay the ham over the top. Serve the salsa separately in a small bowl.

Wild Mushroom Salad with Parma Ham

Autumn provides a wealth of ingredients for the salad maker. Most treasured of all are wild mushrooms, found mainly in deciduous woodland. If you are not familiar with edible species, larger supermarkets and specialist delicatessens often sell a wide range.

INGREDIENTS

Serves 4

175 g/6 oz Parma ham, thickly sliced

45 ml/3 tbsp butter

450 g/1 lb wild or cultivated mushrooms such as chanterelles, field blewits, oyster mushrooms, champignons de Paris, sliced

60 ml/4 tbsp brandy

½ oakleaf lettuce

½ frisée lettuce

15 ml/1 tbsp walnut oil

salt and ground black pepper

For the herb pancake

45 ml/3 tbsp plain flour

75 ml/5 tbsp milk

1 egg, plus 1 egg yolk

60 ml/4 tbsp grated Parmesan cheese

45 ml/3 tbsp chopped fresh mixed herbs such as parsley, thyme, tarragon, marjoram, chives

salt and ground black pepper

1 To make the pancakes, combine the flour with the milk in a measuring jug. Beat in the egg and egg yolk with the Parmesan cheese, herbs and seasoning. Place a non-stick frying pan over a steady heat. Pour in enough mixture to coat the bottom of the pan.

2 When the batter has set, turn the pancake over and cook briefly on the other side. Turn the pancake out and leave to cool. Continue until you have used all the batter.

3 Roll the pancakes together and cut into 1 cm/½ in ribbons. Cut the Parma ham into similar-sized ribbons and toss together with the pancake ribbons.

4 Heat the butter in a frying pan until it begins to foam. Add the mushrooms and cook for 6–8 minutes. Add the brandy and ignite with a match. The flames will subside when the alcohol has burnt off. Moisten the salad leaves with walnut oil and distribute among four serving plates. Place the ham and pancake ribbons in the centre, spoon on the mushrooms, season and serve warm.

Beef and Herby Pasta Salad

Lean, tender beef is marinated with ginger and garlic, then lightly grilled and served warm with a herby pasta salad.

INGREDIENTS

Serves 6

450 g/1 lb beef fillet

450 g/1 lb fresh tagliatelle with sun-dried
   tomatoes and herbs

115 g/4 oz cherry tomatoes

½ cucumber

For the marinade

15 ml/1 tbsp soy sauce

15 ml/1 tbsp sherry

5 ml/1 tsp grated fresh root ginger

1 garlic clove, crushed

For the herb dressing

30–45 ml/2–3 tbsp horseradish sauce

150 ml/¼ pint/⅔ cup plain yogurt

1 garlic clove, crushed

30–45 ml/2–3 tbsp chopped fresh mixed
   herbs such as chives, parsley, thyme

salt and ground black pepper

2 Preheat the grill. Lift the fillet out of the marinade and pat it dry with kitchen paper. Place the fillet on a grill rack and grill for 8 minutes on each side, basting with the marinade during cooking.

3 Transfer the fillet to a plate, cover with foil and leave to stand for 20 minutes.

4 To make the herb dressing, put all the ingredients into a bowl and mix thoroughly. Cook the pasta until it is *al dente*, drain thoroughly, rinse under cold water and leave to dry.

5 Cut the cherry tomatoes in half. Cut the cucumber in half lengthways, scoop out the seeds with a teaspoon and slice the flesh thinly into crescents.

6 Put the pasta, tomatoes, cucumber and dressing into a mixing bowl and toss to coat. Slice the beef and arrange on individual serving plates with the pasta salad. Serve warm.

1 To make the marinade, mix all the ingredients together in a shallow dish. Add the beef fillet and turn to coat well. Cover with clear film and leave for 30 minutes to allow the flavours to penetrate the meat.

Rockburger Salad with Sesame Croûtons

This salad plays on the ingredients that make up the all-American beefburger in a sesame seed bun. Inside the burger is a layer of Roquefort, the blue ewe's-milk cheese from France.

INGREDIENTS

Serves 4

900 g/2 lb lean minced beef

1 egg

1 medium onion, finely chopped

10 ml/2 tsp Dijon mustard

2.5 ml/½ tsp celery salt

115 g/4 oz Roquefort or other blue cheese

1 large sesame seed loaf

45 ml/3 tbsp olive oil

1 small iceberg lettuce

50 g/2 oz rocket or watercress leaves

120 ml/4 fl oz/½ cup French Dressing

4 ripe tomatoes, quartered

4 large spring onions, sliced

ground black pepper

1 Place the minced beef, egg, onion, mustard, celery salt and pepper in a mixing bowl. Combine thoroughly. Divide the mixture into 16 equal portions.

2 Flatten the pieces between two sheets of polythene or waxed paper to form 13 cm/5 in rounds.

3 Place 15 g/½ oz of the blue cheese on eight of the burgers. Sandwich with the remaining burgers and press the edges firmly. Store between sheets of polythene or waxed paper and chill until ready to cook.

4 To make the sesame croûtons, preheat the grill to a moderate temperature. Remove the sesame seed crust from the loaf, then cut the crust into short fingers. Moisten with olive oil and toast evenly for 10–15 minutes.

5 Grill the burgers at the same temperature for 10 minutes, turning once.

6 Toss the salad leaves with the French Dressing, then distribute between four large serving plates. Place two rockburgers in the centre of each plate and arrange the tomatoes, spring onions and sesame croûtons around the edge.

COOK'S TIP

If you can't find a sesame seed loaf use a French stick. Cut the stick into slices of around 1 cm/½ in, brush with olive oil and place on a baking tray. Bake in the oven on a low heat for around 15 minutes until the bread rounds are crisp and golden.

FRUIT SALADS

Fresh Fruit Salad

This basic fruit salad is always welcome, especially after a rich main course. It is endlessly adaptable – when peaches and strawberries are out of season, use bananas and grapes, or any other fruit.

INGREDIENTS

Serves 6

2 apples

2 oranges

2 peaches

16–20 strawberries

30 ml/2 tbsp lemon juice

15–30 ml/1–2 tbsp orange flower water

icing sugar (optional)

a few fresh mint leaves, to decorate

1 Peel and core the apples and cut into thin slices. Peel the oranges with a sharp knife, removing all the pith, and segment them, catching the juice in a bowl.

2 Plunge the peaches for 1 minute in boiling water, peel away the skin and cut the flesh into thick slices, discarding the stone.

3 Hull the strawberries and halve or quarter if larger. Place all the fruit in a large serving bowl.

4 Blend together the lemon juice, orange flower water and orange juice. Taste and add a little icing sugar to sweeten, if liked. Pour the fruit juice mixture over the salad and serve decorated with mint leaves.

Dried Fruit Salad

This wonderful combination of fresh and dried fruit makes an excellent dessert throughout the year. Use frozen raspberries and blackberries during the winter months.

INGREDIENTS

Serves 4

115 g/4 oz/½ cup dried apricots

115 g/4 oz/½ cup dried peaches

1 pear

1 apple

1 orange

115 g/4 oz/⅔ cup mixed raspberries
   and blackberries

1 cinnamon stick

50 g/2 oz/¼ cup caster sugar

15 ml/1 tbsp clear honey

15 ml/1 tbsp lemon juice

1 Soak the dried apricots and peaches in water for 1–2 hours, until plump, then drain and halve or quarter. Peel and core the pear and apple and cut into cubes.

2 Peel the orange with a sharp knife, removing all the pith, and cut into wedges. Place all the fruit in a large saucepan with the raspberries and blackberries.

3 Add 600 ml/1 pint/2½ cups water, the cinnamon stick, sugar and honey and bring to the boil. Cover and simmer very gently for 10–12 minutes, then remove the pan from the heat.

4 Stir in the lemon juice. Allow to cool, then transfer to a bowl and chill in the fridge for 1–2 hours before serving.

Italian Fruit Salad and Ice Cream

If you visit Italy in the summer, you will find little pavement fruit shops selling small dishes of macerated soft fruits, which are delectable on their own, but also make a wonderful ice cream.

INGREDIENTS

Serves 6

900 g/2 lb mixed summer fruits such as
    strawberries, raspberries, loganberries,
    redcurrants, blueberries, peaches,
    apricots, plums, melons
juice of 3–4 oranges
juice of 1 lemon
15 ml/1 tbsp liquid pear and apple
    concentrate
60 ml/4 tbsp whipping cream
30 ml/2 tbsp orange liqueur (optional)
fresh mint sprigs, to decorate

1 Prepare the fruit according to type. Cut it into reasonably small pieces.

2 Put the fruit into a serving bowl and pour over enough orange juice to cover. Add the lemon juice and chill for 2 hours.

3 Set half the macerated fruit aside to serve as it is. Purée the remainder in a blender or food processor.

4 Gently warm the pear and apple concentrate and stir into the fruit purée. Whip the cream and fold it in, then add the liqueur, if using.

5 Churn the mixture in an ice-cream maker. Alternatively, place it in a suitable container for freezing. Freeze until ice crystals form around the edge, then beat the mixture until smooth.

6 Repeat the process once or twice, then freeze until firm.

7 Allow to soften slightly in the fridge before serving with the fruit in scoops decorated with sprigs of mint.

COOK'S TIP

The macerated fruit also makes a delicious drink. Purée in a blender or food processor, then press through a sieve.

Cool Green Fruit Salad

A sophisticated, simple fruit salad for any time of the year.

INGREDIENTS

Serves 6

3 Ogen or Galia melons

115 g/4 oz seedless green grapes

2 kiwi fruit

1 star fruit

1 green-skinned apple

1 lime

175 ml/6 fl oz/¾ cup sparkling grape juice

1 Cut the melons in half and remove the seeds. Keeping the shells intact, scoop out the flesh with a melon baller, or scoop it out with a spoon and cut into bite-size cubes. Reserve the melon shells.

2 Remove any stems from the grapes and, if they are large, cut them in half. Peel and chop the kiwi fruit. Thinly slice the star fruit. Core and thinly slice the apple and place in a mixing bowl with the melon, grapes, kiwi fruit and star fruit.

3 Thinly pare the rind from the lime and cut it in fine strips. Blanch the lime strips in boiling water for 30 seconds, drain and rinse in cold water. Squeeze the juice from the lime and toss the juice into the bowl of fruit.

4 Spoon the prepared fruit into the reserved melon shells and chill the shells in the fridge until required. Just before serving, spoon the sparkling grape juice over the fruit and scatter with the strips of lime rind.

COOK'S TIP

On a hot summer's day, serve the filled melon shells nestling on a platter of crushed ice to keep them beautifully cool.

Winter Fruit Salad

This is a colourful, refreshing and nutritious fruit salad, which is ideal served with Greek yogurt or cream.

INGREDIENTS

Serves 6

225 g/8 oz can pineapple cubes in
    fruit juice
200 ml/7 fl oz/scant 1 cup freshly
    squeezed orange juice
200 ml/7 fl oz/scant 1 cup unsweetened
    apple juice
30 ml/2 tbsp orange or apple liqueur
30 ml/2 tbsp clear honey (optional)
2 oranges, peeled
2 green-skinned apples, chopped
2 pears, chopped
4 plums, stoned and chopped
12 fresh dates, stoned and chopped
115 g/4 oz/½ cup ready-to-eat dried
    apricots
fresh mint sprigs, to decorate

1 Drain the pineapple, reserving the juice. Put the pineapple juice, orange juice, apple juice, liqueur and honey, if using, in a large serving bowl and stir.

COOK'S TIP

Use other unsweetened fruit juices such as pink grapefruit and pineapple juice in place of the orange and apple juice.

2 Segment the oranges, catching any juice in the bowl. Put the orange segments and pineapple in the fruit juice mixture.

3 Add the chopped apples and pears to the bowl.

4 Stir in the plums, dates and dried apricots, cover and chill for several hours. Decorate with fresh mint sprigs to serve.

Italian Fruit Salad and Ice Cream

If you visit Italy in the summer, you will find little pavement fruit shops selling small dishes of macerated soft fruits, which are delectable on their own, but also make a wonderful ice cream.

INGREDIENTS

Serves 6

900 g/2 lb mixed summer fruits such as
    strawberries, raspberries, loganberries,
    redcurrants, blueberries, peaches,
    apricots, plums, melons

juice of 3–4 oranges

juice of 1 lemon

15 ml/1 tbsp liquid pear and apple
    concentrate

60 ml/4 tbsp whipping cream

30 ml/2 tbsp orange liqueur (optional)

fresh mint sprigs, to decorate

1 Prepare the fruit according to type. Cut it into reasonably small pieces.

2 Put the fruit into a serving bowl and pour over enough orange juice to cover. Add the lemon juice and chill for 2 hours.

3 Set half the macerated fruit aside to serve as it is. Purée the remainder in a blender or food processor.

4 Gently warm the pear and apple concentrate and stir into the fruit purée. Whip the cream and fold it in, then add the liqueur, if using.

5 Churn the mixture in an ice-cream maker. Alternatively, place it in a suitable container for freezing. Freeze until ice crystals form around the edge, then beat the mixture until smooth.

6 Repeat the process once or twice, then freeze until firm.

7 Allow to soften slightly in the fridge before serving with the fruit in scoops decorated with sprigs of mint.

COOK'S TIP

The macerated fruit also makes a delicious drink. Purée in a blender or food processor, then press through a sieve.

Watermelon, Ginger and Grapefruit Salad

*This pretty, pink combination is
very light and refreshing for any
summer meal.*

INGREDIENTS

Serves 4

450 g/1 lb/2 cups watermelon flesh

2 ruby or pink grapefruit

2 pieces stem ginger and 30 ml/2 tbsp of
the syrup

1 Remove any seeds from the
watermelon and cut the flesh
into bite-size chunks.

2 Using a small, sharp knife, cut
away all the peel and white
pith from the grapefruit and
carefully lift out the segments,
catching any juice in a bowl.

COOK'S TIP

Toss the fruits gently – grapefruit
segments will break up easily
and the appearance of the dish
will be spoiled.

3 Finely chop the stem ginger
and place in a serving bowl
with the melon cubes and
grapefruit segments, adding the
reserved juice.

4 Spoon over the ginger syrup
and toss the fruits lightly to
mix. Chill before serving.

Fresh Fruit with Mango Coulis

Fruit sauce, or coulis, became very fashionable in the 1970s with nouvelle cuisine. This bright, flavourful sauce is easy to prepare and ideal for making a simple fruit salad seem special.

INGREDIENTS

Serves 6

1 large ripe mango, peeled, stoned
    and chopped
rind of 1 unwaxed orange
juice of 3 oranges
caster sugar, to taste
2 peaches
2 nectarines
1 small mango, peeled
2 plums
1 pear or ½ small melon
juice of 1 lemon
25–50 g/1–2 oz heaped tbsp wild
    strawberries (optional)
25–50 g/1–2 oz heaped tbsp raspberries
25–50 g/1–2 oz heaped tbsp blueberries
small fresh mint sprigs, to decorate

1 In a food processor fitted with a metal blade, blend the large mango until smooth. Add the orange rind and juice and sugar to taste and process again until very smooth. Press through a sieve into a bowl and chill.

2 Slice and stone the peaches, nectarines, small mango and plums. Quarter the pear and remove the core or, if using, slice the melon thinly and remove the skin.

3 Place the sliced fruits on a large plate, sprinkle with the lemon juice and chill, covered with clear film, for up to 3 hours before serving. (Some fruits discolour if cut too far ahead of time.)

4 To serve, arrange the sliced fruits on serving plates, spoon the berries on top, drizzle with a little mango coulis and decorate with mint sprigs. Serve the remaining coulis separately.

Fruits-of-the-Tropics Salad

*This is a creamy, exotic fruit salad
flavoured with coconut and spices.*

INGREDIENTS

Serves 4–6

1 medium pineapple

400 g/14 oz can guava halves in syrup

2 medium bananas, sliced

1 large mango, peeled, stoned and diced

115 g/4 oz stem ginger and 30 ml/2 tbsp of
   the syrup

60 ml/4 tbsp thick coconut milk

10 ml/2 tsp sugar

2.5 ml/^{1}/$_2$ tsp grated nutmeg

2.5 ml/^{1}/$_2$ tsp ground cinnamon

strips of coconut, to decorate

1 Peel, core and cube the
  pineapple, and place in a
serving bowl. Drain the guavas,
reserving the syrup, and chop. Add
the guavas to the bowl with one of
the bananas and the mango.

2 Chop the stem ginger and add
  to the pineapple mixture.

3 Pour the 30 ml/2 tbsp of the
  ginger syrup and the reserved
guava syrup into a blender or food
processor and add the remaining
banana, the coconut milk and the
sugar. Blend to make a smooth,
creamy purée.

4 Pour the banana and coconut
  purée over the fruit and add
a little grated nutmeg and a
sprinkling of cinnamon on top.
Serve chilled, decorated with strips
of coconut.

Exotic Fruit Salad

A variety of fruits can be used for this salad depending on what is available. Look out for fresh mandarin oranges, star fruit, pawpaw, Cape gooseberries and passion fruit.

INGREDIENTS

Serves 4

75 g/3 oz/scant ½ cup sugar

30 ml/2 tbsp stem ginger syrup

2 pieces star anise

2.5 cm/1 in cinnamon stick

1 clove

juice of ½ lemon

2 fresh mint sprigs

1 mango

2 bananas

8 lychees, fresh or canned

225 g/8 oz/2 cups strawberries

2 pieces stem ginger, cut into sticks

1 medium pineapple

1 Place the sugar in a saucepan and add 300ml/½ pint/1¼ cups water, the ginger syrup, spices, lemon juice and mint. Bring to the boil and simmer for 3 minutes. Strain into a large bowl.

2 Remove both the top and bottom from the mango and remove the outer skin. Stand the mango on one end and remove the flesh in two pieces either side of the flat stone. Slice evenly and add to the syrup. Add the bananas, lychees, strawberries and ginger. Chill until ready to serve.

3 Cut the pineapple in half down the centre. Loosen the flesh with a small, serrated knife and remove to form two boat shapes. Cut the pineapple flesh into large chunks and place in the cooled syrup.

4 Spoon the fruit salad carefully into the pineapple halves and bring to the table on a large serving dish or board. There will be enough fruit salad left over to refill the pineapple halves for a second serving.

Melon and Strawberry Salad

A beautiful and colourful fruit salad, this is equally suitable to serve as a refreshing appetizer or to round off a meal.

INGREDIENTS

Serves 4

1 Galia melon

1 honeydew melon

½ watermelon

225 g/8 oz/2 cups strawberries

15 ml/1 tbsp lemon juice

15 ml/1 tbsp clear honey

15 ml/1 tbsp chopped fresh mint

1 fresh mint sprig (optional)

1 Prepare the melons by cutting them in half and discarding the seeds. Use a melon baller to scoop out the flesh into balls or alternatively a knife to cut it into cubes. Place these in a fruit bowl.

2 Rinse and hull the strawberries, cut in half and add to the melon balls or cubes.

COOK'S TIP
∼

Use whichever melons are available: replace Galia with cantaloupe or watermelon with Charentais, for example. Try to choose three melons with a variation in colour for an attractive effect.

3 Mix together the lemon juice and honey and add 15 ml/ 1 tbsp water to make it easier to spoon over the fruit. Mix into the fruit gently.

4 Sprinkle the chopped mint over the top of the fruit. Serve the fruit salad decorated with the mint sprig, if wished.

Blueberry, Orange and Lavender Salad

Delicate blueberries feature here in a simple salad of sharp oranges and sweet little meringues flavoured with fresh lavender.

INGREDIENTS

Serves 4

6 oranges

350 g/12 oz/3 cups blueberries

8 fresh lavender sprigs, to decorate

For the meringue

2 egg whites

115 g/4 oz/generous ½ cup caster sugar

5 ml/1 tsp fresh lavender flowers

1 Preheat the oven to 140°C/ 275°F/Gas 1. Line a baking sheet with six layers of newspaper and cover with non-stick baking parchment. To make the meringue, whisk the egg whites in a large mixing bowl until they hold their weight on the whisk. Add the sugar a little at a time, whisking thoroughly before each addition. Fold in the lavender flowers.

2 Spoon the lavender meringue into a piping bag fitted with a 5 mm/¼ in plain nozzle. Pipe as many small buttons of meringue on to the prepared baking sheet as you can. Dry the meringues near the bottom of the oven for 1½–2 hours.

3 To segment the oranges, remove the peel from the top, bottom and sides with a serrated knife. Loosen the segments by cutting with a paring knife between the flesh and the membranes, holding the fruit over a bowl.

4 Arrange the orange segments on four plates.

5 Combine the blueberries with the lavender meringues and pile in the centre of each plate. Decorate with sprigs of lavender and serve.

Fresh Fig, Apple and Date Salad

Sweet Mediterranean figs and dates combine especially well with crisp dessert apples. A hint of almond serves to unite the flavours.

INGREDIENTS

Serves 4

6 large apples

juice of ½ lemon

175 g/6 oz/generous 1 cup fresh dates

25 g/1 oz white marzipan

5 ml/1 tsp orange flower water

60 ml/4 tbsp plain yogurt

4 ripe green or purple figs

4 almonds, toasted

1 Core the apples. Slice thinly, then cut into fine matchsticks. Moisten with lemon juice to keep them white.

2 Remove the stones from the dates and cut the flesh into fine strips, then combine them with the apple slices.

3 Soften the marzipan with the orange flower water and combine with the yogurt. Mix well.

4 Pile the apples and dates in the centre of four serving plates. Remove the stem from each of the figs and divide the fruit into quarters without cutting right through the base. Squeeze the base with the thumb and forefinger of each hand to open up the fig.

5 Place a fig in the centre of each fruit salad, spoon in the yogurt filling and decorate with a toasted almond.

Blackberry Salad with Rose Granita

The blackberry is a member of the rose family and combines especially well with rose water. Here a rose syrup is frozen into a granita and served over strips of white meringue.

INGREDIENTS

Serves 4

150 g/5 oz/⅔ cup caster sugar
1 fresh red rose, petals finely chopped
5 ml/1 tsp rose water
10 ml/2 tsp lemon juice
450 g/1 lb/2⅔ cups blackberries
icing sugar, for dusting
fresh rose petals, to decorate

For the meringue
2 egg whites
115 g/4 oz/generous ½ cup caster sugar

1 To make the granita, bring 150 ml/¼ pint/⅔ cup water to the boil in a stainless-steel or enamel saucepan. Add the sugar and rose petals, then simmer for 5 minutes.

2 Strain the syrup into a deep metal tray, add a further 450 ml/¾ pint/scant 2 cups water, the rose water and lemon juice and leave to cool. Freeze the mixture for 3 hours, or until solid.

3 Meanwhile preheat the oven to 140°C/275°F/Gas 1. Line a baking sheet with six layers of newspaper and cover with non-stick baking parchment.

4 To make the meringue, whisk the egg whites until they hold their weight on the whisk. Add the caster sugar a little at a time, and whisk until firm.

COOK'S TIP

Blackberries are widely cultivated from late spring to autumn and are usually large, plump and sweet. The finest wild blackberries have a bitter edge and a strong depth of flavour – best appreciated with a sprinkling of sugar.

5 Spoon the meringue into a piping bag fitted with a 1 cm/½ in plain nozzle. Pipe the meringue in lengths across the paper-lined baking sheet. Dry the meringue near the bottom of the oven for 1½–2 hours.

6 Break the meringue into 5 cm/2 in lengths and place three or four pieces on each of four large serving plates. Pile the blackberries next to the meringue.

7 With a tablespoon, scrape the granita finely. Shape into ovals and place over the meringue. Dust with icing sugar, decorate with rose petals, and serve.

Raspberries with Mango Custard

This remarkable salad unites the sharp quality of fresh raspberries with a special custard made from rich, fragrant mangoes.

INGREDIENTS

Serves 4

1 large mango

3 egg yolks

30 ml/2 tbsp caster sugar

10 ml/2 tsp cornflour

200 ml/7 fl oz/scant 1 cup milk

8 fresh mint sprigs, to decorate

For the raspberry sauce

450 g/1 lb/2⅔ cups raspberries

45 ml/3 tbsp caster sugar

2 For the custard, combine the egg yolks, sugar, cornflour and 30 ml/2 tbsp of the milk smoothly in a small bowl.

5 Pour the custard into a food processor, add the chopped mango and blend until smooth. Allow the custard to cool.

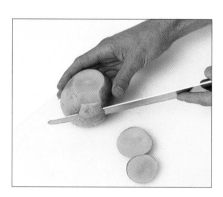

1 To prepare the mango, remove the top and bottom with a serrated knife. Cut away the outer skin, then remove the flesh by cutting either side of the flat central stone. Save half of the mango flesh for decoration and roughly chop the remainder.

3 Rinse a small saucepan with cold water to prevent the milk from catching. Bring the rest of the milk to the boil in the pan, pour it over the ingredients in the bowl and stir evenly.

6 To make the raspberry sauce, place 350 g/12 oz/2 cups of the raspberries in a stain-resistant saucepan. Add the sugar, soften over a gentle heat and simmer for 5 minutes. Rub the fruit through a fine nylon sieve to remove the seeds. Allow to cool.

7 Spoon the raspberry sauce and mango custard into two pools on four serving plates. Slice the reserved mango and fan out or arrange in a pattern over the raspberry sauce. Scatter the remaining raspberries over the mango custard. Decorate each plate with two sprigs of mint and serve.

4 Strain the mixture through a sieve back into the saucepan, stir to simmering point and allow the mixture to thicken.

COOK'S TIP

Mangoes are ripe when they yield to gentle pressure. Some varieties show a red-gold or yellow flush when they are ready to eat.

Pineapple Crush with Strawberries and Lychees

The sweet, tropical flavours of pineapple and lychees combine well with richly scented strawberries to make this a most refreshing salad.

INGREDIENTS

Serves 4

2 small pineapples

450 g/1 lb/4 cups strawberries

400 g/14 oz can lychees

45 ml/3 tbsp kirsch or white rum

30 ml/2 tbsp icing sugar

1 Remove the crowns from both pineapples by twisting sharply. Reserve the leaves for decoration.

2 Cut both pineapples in half diagonally using a large, serrated knife.

3 Cut around the flesh inside the skin of both pineapples with a small, serrated knife, keeping the skin intact. Remove the core from the pineapple and discard. Chop the flesh. Reserve the skins.

4 Hull the strawberries and gently combine with the pineapple and lychees, taking care not to damage the fruit.

5 Mix the kirsch or rum with the icing sugar, pour over the fruit and freeze for 45 minutes.

6 Turn out the fruit into the pineapple skins, decorate with the reserved pineapple leaves and serve.

COOK'S TIP

A ripe pineapple will resist pressure when squeezed and will have a sweet, fragrant smell. In winter freezing conditions can cause the flesh to blacken.

Muscat Grape Frappé

The flavour and perfume of the Muscat grape is rarely more enticing than when captured in this sophisticated, icy-cool salad. Because of its alcohol content this dish is not suitable for young children.

INGREDIENTS

Serves 4

½ bottle Muscat wine, Beaumes de Venise, Frontignan or Rivesaltes

450 g/1 lb Muscat grapes

1 Pour the wine into a stainless-steel or enamel tray, add 150 ml/¼ pint/⅔ cup water and freeze for 3 hours, or until the wine is completely solid.

2 Remove the seeds from the grapes with a pair of tweezers. If you have time, you can also peel the grapes. Scrape across the frozen wine with a tablespoon to make a fine ice. Combine the grapes with the ice, spoon into four shallow glasses and serve.

Grapefruit Salad with Campari and Orange

The bitter-sweet flavour of Campari combines especially well with citrus fruit such as grapefruit and oranges. Because of its alcohol content, this dish is not suitable for young children.

INGREDIENTS

Serves 4

45 ml/3 tbsp caster sugar

60 ml/4 tbsp Campari

30 ml/2 tbsp lemon juice

4 grapefruit

5 oranges

4 fresh mint sprigs, to decorate

1 Bring 150 ml/¼ pint/⅔ cup water to the boil in a small saucepan, add the sugar and simmer until dissolved. Transfer to a bowl, allow to cool, then add the Campari and lemon juice. Chill until ready to serve.

2 Cut the peel from the top, bottom and sides of the grapefruit and oranges with a serrated knife. Segment the fruit into a bowl by slipping a small paring knife between the flesh and the membranes. Combine the fruit with the Campari syrup and chill.

3 Spoon the salad into four dishes, decorate with a sprig of fresh mint and serve.

COOK'S TIP

When buying citrus fruit, choose brightly-coloured varieties that feel heavy for their size.

Fruit Kebabs with Mango and Yogurt Sauce

To enjoy these mixed fruit kebabs, dip them into the refreshingly minty mango and yogurt sauce.

Serves 4

½ pineapple, peeled, cored and cubed

2 kiwi fruit, peeled and cubed

150 g/5 oz/scant 1 cup strawberries, hulled and cut in half lengthways if large

½ mango, peeled, stoned and cubed

For the sauce

120 ml/4 fl oz/½ cup fresh mango purée, made from 1–1½ peeled and stoned mangoes

120 ml/4 fl oz/½ cup thick plain yogurt

5 ml/1 tsp sugar

few drops of vanilla essence

15 ml/1 tbsp finely shredded fresh mint leaves

1 fresh mint sprig, to decorate

1 To make the sauce, beat together the mango purée, yogurt, sugar and vanilla with an electric hand mixer.

2 Stir in the shredded mint. Cover the sauce and chill until required.

3 Thread the fruit on to twelve 15 cm/6 in wooden skewers, alternating the pineapple, kiwi fruit, strawberries and mango.

4 Transfer the mango and yogurt sauce to an attractive bowl, decorate with a mint sprig and place in the centre of a large serving platter. Surround with the kebabs and serve.

Tropical Fruits in Cinnamon Syrup

These glistening fruits are best prepared a day in advance to allow the flavours to develop and mingle.

Serves 6

450 g/1 lb/2¼ cups caster sugar

1 cinnamon stick

1 large or 2 medium pawpaws (about 675 g/1½ lb) peeled, seeded and cut lengthways into thin pieces

1 large or 2 medium mangoes (about 675 g/1½ lb) peeled, stoned and cut lengthways into thin pieces

1 large or 2 small star fruit (about 225 g/ 8 oz) thinly sliced

1 Sprinkle one third of the sugar over the bottom of a large saucepan. Add the cinnamon stick and half of the pawpaw, mango and star fruit pieces.

2 Sprinkle half of the remaining sugar over the fruit pieces in the pan. Add the remaining fruit and sprinkle with the remaining sugar.

3 Cover the pan and cook the fruit over medium heat for 35–45 minutes, until the sugar dissolves completely. Shake the pan occasionally, but do not stir or the fruit will collapse.

4 Uncover the pan and simmer for about 10 minutes, until the fruit begins to appear translucent. Remove the pan from the heat and allow to cool. Discard the cinnamon stick.

5 Transfer the fruit and syrup to a bowl, cover and refrigerate overnight before serving.

Banana and Mascarpone

If you are a fan of cold banana custard, you'll love this recipe. It is a grown-up version of an old favourite. No one will guess that the secret is ready-made custard sauce.

INGREDIENTS

Serves 4-6

250 g/9 oz/generous 1 cup mascarpone
    cheese
300 ml/½ pint/1¼ cups fresh ready-made
    custard sauce
150 ml/¼ pint/⅔ cup Greek yogurt
4 bananas
juice of 1 lime
50 g/2 oz/½ cup pecan nuts,
    coarsely chopped
120 ml/4 fl oz/½ cup maple syrup

1 Combine the mascarpone, custard sauce and yogurt in a large bowl and beat together until smooth. Make this mixture up to several hours ahead, if you like. Cover and chill, then stir before using.

2 Slice the bananas diagonally and place in a separate bowl. Pour over the lime juice and toss together until the bananas are coated in the juice.

3 Divide half the custard mixture among four to six dessert glasses and top each portion with a generous spoonful of the banana mixture.

4 Spoon the remaining custard mixture into the glasses and top with the rest of the bananas. Scatter the nuts over the top. Drizzle maple syrup over each dessert and chill for 30 minutes before serving.

Bananas with Lime and Cardamom

Cardamom and bananas go together perfectly, and this luxurious dessert makes an original treat.

INGREDIENTS

Serves 4

6 small bananas
50 g/2 oz/¼ cup butter
seeds from 4 cardamom
    pods, crushed
50 g/2 oz/½ cup flaked almonds
thinly pared rind and juice
    of 2 limes
50 g/2 oz/⅓ cup light
    muscovado sugar
30 ml/2 tbsp dark rum
vanilla ice cream, to serve

1 Peel the bananas and cut them in half lengthways. Heat half the butter in a large frying pan. Add half the bananas, and cook until the undersides are golden. Turn carefully, using a fish slice. Cook until golden all over.

2 Once cooked, transfer the bananas to a heatproof serving dish. Cook the remaining bananas in the same way.

3 Melt the remaining butter, then add the cardamom seeds and almonds. Cook, stirring until the almonds are golden.

4 Stir in the lime rind and juice, then the sugar. Cook, stirring, until the mixture is smooth, bubbling and slightly reduced. Stir in the rum. Pour the sauce over the bananas and serve immediately, with vanilla ice cream.

Melon Trio with Ginger Biscuits

The eye-catching colours of these three different melons really make this dessert, while the crisp biscuits provide a perfect contrast in terms of texture.

INGREDIENTS

Serves 4

¼ watermelon

½ honeydew melon

½ charentais melon

60 ml/4 tbsp stem ginger syrup

For the biscuits

25 g/1 oz/2 tbsp unsalted butter

25 g/1 oz/2 tbsp caster sugar

5 ml/1 tsp clear honey

25 g/1 oz/¼ cup plain flour

25 g/1 oz/¼ cup luxury glacé
   mixed fruit, finely chopped

1 piece of stem ginger in syrup, drained
   and finely chopped

30 ml/2 tbsp flaked almonds

1 Remove the seeds from the melons, cut them into wedges, then slice off the rind. Cut all the flesh into chunks and mix in a bowl. Stir in the ginger syrup, cover and chill until ready to serve.

2 Meanwhile, make the biscuits. Preheat the oven to 180°C/350°F/Gas 4. Heat the butter, sugar and honey in a saucepan until melted. Remove from the heat and stir in the remaining ingredients.

3 Line a baking sheet with non-stick baking paper. Space four spoonfuls of the mixture on the paper at regular intervals, leaving plenty of room for spreading. Flatten the mixture slightly into rounds and bake for 15 minutes or until the tops are golden.

4 Let the biscuits cool on the baking sheet for 1 minute, then lift each one in turn, using a fish slice, and drape over a rolling pin to cool and harden. Repeat with the remaining ginger mixture to make eight biscuits in all.

5 Serve the melon chunks with some of the syrup and the ginger biscuits.

COOK'S TIP

For an even prettier effect, scoop the melon flesh into balls with the large end of a melon baller.

Jamaican Fruit Trifle

This trifle is actually based on a Caribbean fool that consists of fruit stirred into thick vanilla-flavoured cream. This version is much less rich, redressing the balance with plenty of fruit and crème fraîche.

INGREDIENTS

Serves 8

1 large sweet pineapple, peeled and cored, about 350 g/12 oz

300 ml/½ pint/1¼ cups double cream

200 ml/7 fl oz/scant 1 cup crème fraîche

60 ml/4 tbsp icing sugar, sifted

10 ml/2 tsp pure vanilla essence

30 ml/2 tbsp white or coconut rum

3 papayas, peeled, seeded and chopped

3 mangoes, peeled, stoned and chopped

thinly pared rind and juice of 1 lime

25 g/1 oz/⅓ cup coarsely shredded or flaked coconut, toasted

1 Cut the pineapple into large chunks, place in a food processor or blender and process briefly until chopped. Tip into a sieve placed over a bowl and leave for 5 minutes so that most of the juice drains from the fruit.

2 Whip the double cream to very soft peaks, then lightly but thoroughly fold in the crème fraîche, sifted icing sugar, vanilla essence and rum.

3 Fold the drained, chopped pineapple into the cream mixture. Place the chopped papayas and mangoes in a large bowl and pour over the lime juice. Gently stir the fruit mixture to combine. Shred the pared lime rind and add to the bowl.

4 Divide the fruit mixture and the pineapple cream among eight dessert plates. Decorate with the lime shreds, toasted coconut and a few small pineapple leaves, if you like, and serve at once.

COOK'S TIP

It is important to let the pineapple purée drain thoroughly, otherwise the pineapple cream will be watery. Don't throw away the drained pineapple juice – mix it with fizzy mineral water for a refreshing drink.

Tropical Fruit Gratin

This out-of-the-ordinary gratin is strictly for grown-ups. A colourful combination of fruit is topped with a simple sabayon before being flashed under the grill.

INGREDIENTS

Serves 4

2 tamarillos

½ sweet pineapple

1 ripe mango

175 g/6 oz/1½ cups blackberries

120 ml/4 fl oz/½ cup sparkling white wine

115 g/4 oz/½ cup caster sugar

6 egg yolks

1 Cut each tamarillo in half lengthways and then into thick slices. Cut the rind and core from the pineapple and take spiral slices off the outside to remove the eyes. Cut the flesh into chunks. Peel the mango, cut it in half and cut the flesh from the stone in slices.

2 Divide all the fruit, including the blackberries, among four 14 cm/5½ in gratin dishes set on a baking sheet and set aside. Heat the wine and sugar in a saucepan until the sugar has dissolved. Bring to the boil and cook for 5 minutes.

3 Put the egg yolks in a large heatproof bowl. Place the bowl over a pan of simmering water and whisk until pale. Slowly pour on the hot sugar syrup, whisking all the time, until the mixture thickens. Preheat the grill.

4 Spoon the mixture over the fruit. Place the baking sheet holding the dishes on a low shelf under the hot grill until the topping is golden. Serve hot.

Grilled Pineapple with Papaya sauce

Pineapple cooked this way takes on a superb flavour and is sensational when served with the papaya sauce.

INGREDIENTS

Serves 6

1 sweet pineapple

melted butter, for greasing and brushing

2 pieces drained stem ginger in syrup, cut into fine matchsticks, plus 30 ml/2 tbsp of the syrup from the jar

30 ml/2 tbsp demerara sugar

pinch of ground cinnamon

fresh mint sprigs, to decorate

For the sauce

1 ripe papaya, peeled and seeded

175ml/6fl oz/¾ cup apple juice

1 Peel the pineapple and take spiral slices off the outside to remove the eyes. Cut it crossways into six slices, each 2.5 cm/1 in thick. Line a baking sheet with a sheet of foil, rolling up the sides to make a rim. Grease the foil with melted butter. Preheat the grill.

2 Arrange the pineapple slices on the lined baking sheet. Brush with butter, then top with the ginger matchsticks, sugar and cinnamon. Drizzle over the stem ginger syrup. Grill for 5–7 minutes or until the slices are golden and lightly charred on top.

3 Meanwhile, make the sauce. Cut a few slices from the papaya and set aside, then purée the rest with the apple juice in a blender or food processor.

4 Press the purée through a sieve placed over a bowl, then stir in any juices from cooking the pineapple. Serve the pineapple slices with a little sauce drizzled around each plate. Decorate with the reserved papaya slices and the mint sprigs.